Menomonie and Dunn County, Wisconsin

VOLUME I. NUMBER 6.

THE

American Sketch Book.

EDITED BY

MRS. BELLA FRENCH.

MENOMONIE

AND

Dunn County, Wisconsin.

LA CROSSE, WIS.
SKETCH BOOK COMPANY, PUBLISHERS,
1875.

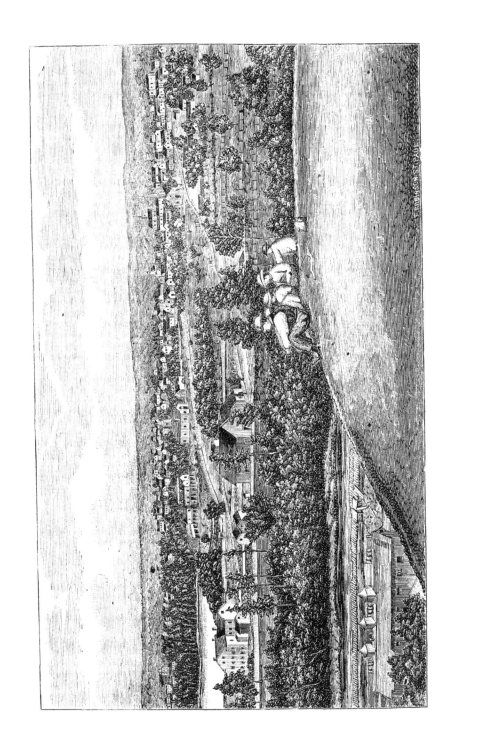

A View of Metophonic Project

Menomonie and Dunn County, Wis.
HISTORICAL SKETCH.

THE INDIANS.

THE land in this section of country was, upon the advent of the whites, claimed by the Chippewa Indians, though it was sometimes invaded by the Sioux. The old settlers say that the beauty, grace, honesty and several other virtues claimed for the dusky sons and daughters of the forest, are all a humbug, and originated in the brain of some love-sick novelist. An Indian maiden was not remarkable for her beauty in olden times any more than she is now. She had little snakey eyes, straight, coarse, black hair; high cheek bones; a flat nose, and a low, retreating forehead. She had her white sister's love of paint, only she sought to improve on nature by using many colors, and more of them. She would appear at times before her lovers with a red forehead, a blue nose, yellow cheeks and a green chin, reversing the color each day to suit her peculiar taste. She was not as particular about the quantity of her wearing apparel as she was about the quality. Her dress in summer generally consisted of a string of beads; in the winter, on account of the severe climate, she was obliged to wear something heavier. She never washed, nor combed her hair. In fact both men and women revelled in filth, as a hog does in the mud.

The love-tales about the Indians also seem to be originated where the idea of Indian beauty is. *The Indian would purchase his squaw from her people, when he made up his mind to have one; and he who

*NOTE.—This statement is contradicted by some of the old settlers, who say that the squaws received presents from lovers, red and white, much the same as the women of our race do; but that the squaws were not trafficked for otherwise, and that they were free to choose for themselves in the matter.

could pay the largest price had the first chance for a bargain. He took as many wives as he wanted, and if he found he could not kill game enough for all, he gave some of them their discharge He put all of the heavy work upon the squaws. Indian admirers say that he did so because it was necessary that his nerves should be steady when taking his aim at game Be this as it may, it is certain that the squaws carried all the burdens, built the wigwams, cut the wood, made the fires and cooked the food, while the master lolled about, drinking and smoking. The Indians have never been believers in women's rights. The squaws have all the rights they want, and do not make any move until commanded by their lords Neither did the Indians improve by mingling with the whites They imitated all the white people's vices, but none of the white people's virtues. They learned readily to drink and gamble, and though the Chippewa language contains no " curse words," they would swear harder in English than any raftsman. More than this, the Chippewas did not take much to the English language. The white people, instead of raising the Indians to their own level, generally descended nearly to a level with them. This intermingling of the races, perhaps, saved much bloodshed and torture, such as have been visited in other localities, for the Indians would not murder their own kinsman, unless greatly exasperated.

The Indians, as a race, though sometimes capable of gratitude, are generally a shrewd, unprincipled people. Mr. L. Bullard, one of the oldest settlers of Menomonie, tells quite an amusing anecdote, illustrative of these characteristics of Indian disposition. In 1849, Mr. Bullard was logging on Hay River, about eighteen miles from where Menomonie now is, and kept a supply store The Indians there constantly coveting the trinkets and liquor which he had on hand for trading purposes, in the fall, brought in their camp-kettles and sold them to Mr Bullard, taking their pay out of the store But when the sugar-making time came, they needed their kettles, and they sent a squaw, whose name was " Old Goose," to borrow them. Mr. Bullard objected, at first, to lending them, but upon Old Goose's pledge of honor to return said kettles in good order, as soon as the sugar season should be over, he reluctantly let them go ; which was done with the understanding that he should receive a certain quantity of sugar for their use. One morning, however, about the close of the sugar-season, Mr. Bullard discovered that the Indians had pulled up their wigwams and departed, bag and baggage, during the previous night, taking along his kettles as well as the sugar which was due him Mr Bullard was angry, so angry that he decided to follow the Indians and recover the camp-kettles Upon his avowing his intentions, a man, George Wilson by name, offered to accompany him, and, strange as it may seem, these two men started in pursuit, without a weapon of any kind with which to defend themselves, in case of an assault. They followed the trail in company, until they found it forked, when they separated, one taking the right and the other the left trail. Mr Bullard had not proceeded far, when he overtook Old Goose's son and another Indian, the former being armed with a shot-gun. The gentleman inquired concerning the squaw and the kettles, but Old Goose's son answered impudently that he knew nothing about either. More exasperated than before, Mr Bullard made the reckless decision to obtain possession of the gun, and making a quick spring, grasped it and tried to wrench it from the Indian, who immediately showed his determination not to give it up   A hot scuffle ensued, during which Indian number two seated himself upon the ground and kept perfectly neutral. Finally the gun was broken in two, each opponent having secured a piece   "I made up my mind then," said the narrator, "that I must kill the Indian to save my life I had the larger piece, and it was the butt end of the gun. I raised this, and made a dash at him, but he sprang backward, crying for mercy, and at the same time, offering me the other piece. I relented in his favor, and taking the offered piece, retraced my steps homeward, closely followed by the Indians. On arriving home, I told my wife the whole story, and then we both began to wonder, somewhat fearfully, what the consequence of my rash act would be. After a while I saw Old Goose's son approaching my dwelling. He knocked at the door and I opened it, knowing full well that it would not do for me to manifest any fear Judge of my surprise, when I tell you that ranged along by the fence, were the missing kettles Stealthily, Old Goose had returned them, and that being done, the Indian had come boldly to demand pay for his gun. 'There are your kettles,' he said in the Chippewa tongue 'We do not steal, nor lie, nor cheat You got mad and broke my gun, and I want to be paid for it '" Upon reflection, Mr Bullard concluded to pay for the gun, as the Indian asked only eight dollars in trade for it, but he also gave the pieces of the broken one back to its owner, knowing that it could be mended with very little work So the quarrel ended, and good feelings were restored.

The Indians, rough, ignorant and uncouth as they are, seem to have always had a tinge of romance about them; and their language is said to be rather flowery. The incidents relating to the sickness, death and burial of Saganash, as told by Mrs. Bullard, is one worthy of a place in this article. These transpired during tht residence of the Bullards on Hay River. Saganash was an old Indian, struck down with consumption, and obliged to leave his tribe, since he could no longer follow it. One of his squaws (he had had three) had departed this life; another had taken her papoose and gone home to her parents, at his desire, as he could not hunt enough for all, but the last and youngest, he kept with him, that she might care for him until the end. On leaving his tribe, Saganash asked permission of the Bullards to build his wigwam near their store for obvious advantages. The permission being granted, he desired Mr. Bullard to take a blue blanket, which he had in his possession, and immediately after his death to give his squaw therefore, sufficient whisky to enable her and his friends to do the mourning business to perfection. Mr. Bullard refused to take the blanket, as it was cold weather, and the Indian needed it; but he promised to furnish the required whisky. Saganash then made a very effective speech, in which he returned thanks to Mr. Bullard, and also portrayed his own misery and poverty. There had been a time when his wigwam was filled with game, when all his squaws and papooses were about him, and when whisky and tobacco were plenty. Now he was obliged to quit his people, to give up one of his squaws, and to depend on his children for support. He wept while he was speaking, and his apparent sorrow so affected his hearers that they resolved to make his few days as pleasant as possible. Thenceforth, until the time of his death, which occurred about four months later, the Bullards visited him daily, and supplied him with the few luxuries which they could command At one time, during his sickness, Saganash fell into a trance, or a fainting fit, and was thought to be dead by his squaw and children; but the whites soon succeeded in restoring animation, and he then related to his wondering friends a story of a visit to the happy hunting ground—a story which proves plainly how belief and education control the vision and thought at such times. The evil spirit had brought him word that the Great Spirit had sent for him, which was a lie. But believing the devil, he had gone to the happy hunting ground, and waited upon God, with whom he had a long conversation, and who kindly informed him that both he and the Bullards should have a place prepared for them when their days on earth should be ended. He described the happy hunting ground as a land around which great guns were stationed, and those guns kept up a never-ending puff, puff, puff, and were continually bringing down the rarest, fattest game that can be imagined. Observing that the two sons of his dead squaw were shedding tears, he told them not to cry, for he had seen their mother, who was engaged in raising corn in the happy hunting ground country,—that the ears were as long as his arm, and the kernels as long as hickory nuts. He then quietly informed his listeners that he was not to die at that time, for God had sent him back, with the request that upon his arrival upon earth, he should have a number of guns fired to proclaim the facts to the inhabitants of the happy hunting ground. So urgent was he in the matter of the firing guns, that the whites humored him by discharging all the fire-arms they had in their possession. Whether the signal was ever recognized by the people of the happy hunting ground, the writer cannot say, but certain it is, the firing was heard by a party of Chippewas encamped three miles distant, and they, believing that the Sioux were on the war-path, fled in dismay from that part of the country. A few weeks later, Saganash died; at which time the squaw received the promised whisky. They buried him where the fire of the wigwam had been kept all winter, that spot being unfrozen. An Indian, related to the dead man, was here at the time, and he made a very flowery and impressive sermon, during which he spoke of the kindness of the whites, declaring in extravagant language that the Chippewas would suffer their ears to be cut off, their tongues torn out and their eyes put out before they would bring any trouble to the settlers on Hay River.

In fact, very few whites suffered from Indian depredation in this section of the country, farther than by petty thefts and like annoyances. There seems to have been but few murders. Two of these are wrapt in mystery, since none know what provoked then. Two men, whose names the writer did not learn, while looking for a mill-site, were set upon by the Indians. Their mutilated bodies were found by some hunters and brought to Menomonie for burial. The murder of William Wickham in 1850 is still fresh in the minds of the old settlers. The Indian, Big Rascal, for some cause or other, had conceived a hatred for Wickham, and one night entered the man's sleeping quarters and stabbed him to the heart. Wickham's bed-fellow, a white man, was obliged to lie all night in a pool of blood by the side of his dead companion, and was threatened with a like fate if he dared to move   There were also two other men, who were searching out pine lands, that were shot by the Indians, while running a canoe up the Red Cedar.   This happened in an early day, and the names of the unfortunate strangers are not remembered by the old settlers.   No other murders by the Indians are on record

SETTLEMENT BY THE WHITES

It is uncertain at what time the pineries on the Red Cedar River were first visited by white people   It is thought that the timber used in constructing the French shanties at Fort Crawford (now known as Prairie du Chien) a century or more ago, was taken from this part of the country ; as saw-pits, having a very ancient appearance, are to be found along the banks of the river   The pits were made for the use of whip-saws   A log was placed across the pit, and two men, one in the pit and one above, with an up-and-down saw, cut it into boards. In 1820, the American Fur Company sent sawyers to this part of the country, and in 1829, companies of men under Lieutenants Gardener and Gale* cut and rafted lumber, from the pineries of the Red Cedar, to complete Fort Crawford.   A Mr. Perkins, of Kentucky, had previously, in 1822, built a mill on the Red Cedar, but it was washed away by a freshet before its completion, and threats from the Indians prevented him from re-building it   Judge Lockwood of Prairie du Chien visited the mill-site in company with the expedition from the fort. The following year, he returned and erected a mill on what is now known as Wilson's Creek.   A year later, he built a second mill, a mile and a half below the first   H. S Allen bought an interest in the mills in 1835, and in 1837 this company-built a third mill still lower down, by about five miles.   In 1839, Lockwood sold out his interest to H. S. Allen.   Five years later a Mr Green bought the upper mill, but sold it soon after to David Black.   For several years, G. S. Branham was associated with H S. Allen in the mill business.   They were known as the firm of Allen & Branham   They sold the middle mill, situated on what is now known as Gilbert's Creek, then called Middle Mill Creek, to Samuel Gilbert & Son, in 1846

Such were the state of affairs when Captain William Wilson, of Fort Madison, Iowa, determined to make an exploring tour through the county in search of a location.   He ascended the Mississippi River by a steamboat to a point known as Nelson's Landing,

*Note — It is claimed by some, that previous to the fitting out of this expedition, another under the command of Jeff Davis, visited the Red Cedar for this same purpose , but this story is not credited as the parties who gave it circulation have been heard to deny its truth

and, learning from Mr. Branham (of the firm of Allen & Branham) with whom he chanced to meet, that good openings were plenty upon the Red Cedar River, he accompanied that gentleman hither. This journey was made on foot, early in the spring of 1846.

Captain Wilson had any amount of ambition, energy and hope, but he was not possessed of much money; and he has long since proved what so often has been disputed—that the three first, if assisted by health, are a fortune in themselves. Finding that an interest in Black's mill was for sale, he made an exploration of fifty miles up the river, to ascertain how the pine would "hold out" The trip was taken in a canoe, with no companion but an Indian guide. He soon became satisfied in regard to the pine-question, and he resolved, then and there, to have an interest in the mill, if by any honorable means he could raise the money required. For this purpose he returned to Fort Madison, where he interviewed John H. Knapp, Esq., a young man who had recently left an eastern college, and who was looking about for an opportunity to invest a small amount of money, a part of which was from his father's estate, and the remainder left him by an uncle in New York. The scheme seemed feasable to Mr. Knapp, and he resolved to look into the matter. He went with Captain Wilson to Black's mill, and finding the property to his liking, concluded to make the purchase. The pair returned to Fort Madison, and there met David Black, with whom they contracted for a half interest in the mill. Shortly after this, Capt. Wilson, accompanied by his family (which consisted of his wife and four children) and Jason Ball and wife, made a trip to their new home, ascending the Chippewa and Red Cedar rivers on a keel boat. (For description of a keel-boat, see page 158 of the current volume of the SKETCH BOOK.) Three weeks later, Mr. Knapp also returned to the mill, bringing with him, on a keel-boat, Mr. and Mrs. Lorenzo Bullard, formerly of Fort Madison, but later of Galena, whom he had engaged to keep the men's boarding-house, and Mrs. Clair and son, Mrs. Bullard's help. He also brought a boat-load of supplies. It may be interesting to some of our readers to know that Mr. Knapp either steered or poled the boat through the entire trip. It was a slow method of traveling at best, and the women must needs have something to pass away the time as well as the men. Upon this particular occasion they brought out a work-basket and employed themselves sewing or knitting. The work-basket contained besides balls of yarn and needle-work, a bottle of bitters belonging to Mr. Bullard. Now it happened that one day little Eugene Bullard, then some three years old, while dancing about the boat, chanced to knock the basket into the river; and as the basket, balls and bottle went gliding over the waves, the women set up a dismal wail, which so smote the tender heart of Mr. Knapp, that he at once sprang overboard to regain the articles. The water was deep and swift, and the young man did not find his self-imposed task an easy one He succeeded in getting the basket and balls, but the bottle of bitters drifted beyond his reach, and in his earnest endeavors to possess it, he gave the people on the boat the idea that he was drowning; and they, in their desire to come to his assistance, upset some other articles, which he also had to swim after and gather in. Knowing that in the new country toward which they were traveling, all their supplies would be needed, he determined to secure every article which was overboard; and as his arms flew about in a livelier manner than ever, the impression that he was drowning gained, and the preparations for assistance began in good earnest. It was not till after having secured basket, balls, bottle and all, he clambered back into the boat, that they could understand just how matters were; and then all parties had a laugh over the affair. Few young men of the present day would jump into swift drift-water to secure a lady's work basket, especially if they had to remain wet all day in consequence, as did Mr. Knapp.

During the same trip the youthful Eugene got into trouble. He made up his mind, one evening while the party were landed in order to get supper, that he would go into the water to bathe. His parents were not willing, but he was a self-willed child, and in he went It was the era of musquitoes. Old settlers say that musquitoes would sweep over the country in masses so thick that they formed a black cloud as they moved. It was only by keeping a constant smoke that the people could live in any measure free from the attacks of those insects. Upon this occasion the wilful youngster had only got fairly stripped and into the water when a cloud of musquitoes settled upon him As their million bills went into his tender flesh, he gave a most unearthly yell, and started for the shore, where he was met by his frightened mother, who put on the slaps (killing musquitoes, of course) thick and fast. His appearance, as he stood by her side, his flesh swollen by the bites, and covered with blood and mashed musquitoes, and his mouth stretched to the utmost capacity in order to give vent to his terrible yells, can better be imagined than described.

The persons already mentioned in this sketch, a few workmen and

two white women, who had been among the Indians so long that they
had about forgotten that they did belong to the Caucassian race,
made up the entire white population for quite a period   The firm
name of the upper mill at this time was Knapp & Black   But Mr
Black died some time during 1846, and J. S Lockwood of Prairie du
Chien, being administrator of Mr. Black's property, made a visit to
the mill for the purpose of investigating matters   Subsequently
Knapp & Wilson bought out the interest of the Black family , and
sometime in the month of September, 1850, Captain Andrew Tainter
became a partner   A new mill, comprising two gang saws and
two rotaries, was erected soon after Captain Tainter's admission into
the mill company   This firm was known as Knapp & Tainter   In
1853, H L Stout of Dubuque, a man of some means, bought an interest in the mills, and the firm then took the name of Knapp, Stout
& Co , which it has ever since retained

It is not the intention of the writer to give the entire history of
this famous company here, as another article will be devoted to that
purpose   A general outline of leading events is what this sketch is
intended to present.

The country about the mills was found to be a magnificent pine
forest, interspersed with hard woods and skirted in places by hard
wood timber-lands   the soil varied and tillable, sandy, with a sub soil
of clay on and near the river banks, and loamy on the table lands ,
and the whole richly watered by pure streams and springs which
offered an abundance of fish With a judgemnt that looked to future
welfare more than to present comforts, the Mill Company, unlike
many other searchers for homes and wealth, instead of being discour-
aged by hardships, or disgusted by the rude society, entered the lands
as fast as they came into market, and thereby laid a foundation for
future wealth and greatness. This company opened the first farm' in
the county, and showed thereby that the soil was very productive, and
in order that the people might be induced to settle on farms, they
bought all the grain raised, for many years, paying a high price for
the same , thus furnishing a good home market and stimulating the
farming interests

There was one benefit, too, arising from the lack of society, looking
at matters from a money-making point of view   Rich dress was not
needed by any one   It is said that a single piece of calico would
furnish all the dresses used by all the women in the neighborhood for
a whole year, and make each a Sunday-go-to-meeting sun-bonnet as
32

well.　The men wore check, and flannel shirts, and outer clothes of coarse cloth.　Men, women and children, from the highest to the lowest, had to work, and no one acted as if he thought himself a little better than were his neighbors.

Supplies for the first settlers were brought up the river by keel-boats in the summer, and by trains on the ice in the winter.　They consisted principally of whisky, pork, beans and flour, the whisky, it is said by some, being largely in excess.　What is true in this respect of this place, is true of the whole country.　The demand for whisky as a commodity is portrayed excellently by Capt. Johnson, in his history of Black River Falls.　It is said that when St. Paul was only an Indian trading-post, it was noticed, one fall, that a Mr. Hartshorn, a trader, while carrying up supplies upon the last boat of the season, had, as part of his cargo, one hundred barrels of whisky, but not a barrel of meat or flour; from which it would seem that the early St. Paulites subsisted almost entirely upon whisky.　People in Dunn County did not suffer actual want, though the food was sometimes coarse and unpalatable　It very often happened that the staves had to be removed from a barrel of flour, and the flour pounded up with an ax, before it could be made into bread　But there was plenty of game, berries and all kinds of wild fruit belonging to these latitudes, and those who were not too indolent to work need have no fears of suffering from lack of food　Still there were hardships which had to be endured while the country was unsettled.　For a time the nearest post-office was at Prairie du Chien, and during that period such of the young men as had left girls behind them, must have had their faith severely tried.　For the first seven years there were no regular wagon roads; and traveling by Indian trails through a then measureless forest, was more romantic than pleasant　There was but little immigration during that period, and the majority of the people who did come, wearied of the hardships attendant upon the life of a pioneer, and returned to their old homes, consequently but little or no society existed, and the cultivated had to seek the companionship of the ignorant and uncouth, or remain isolated from their fellow beings　So the mind, perhaps, knew more of want than did the body.　There were, however, times when the supplies fell short, and when the rifles brought down only muskrats; and those times are looked upon by the old settlers as the hardest ones that they had to endure.　The prejudice against those animals had more to do with making the people feel in actual want, when obliged to eat the flesh than was really necessary; since the uninitiated would partake of it with a relish, and be under the impression that they were eating squirrel-stew. Neither did the old settlers here suffer from attacks of the Indians, as the pioneers in other parts of the Union have done. True, there were occasional battles among Sioux and the Chippewas, and sometimes hard feelings between the whites and the Indians; the settlers very often suffered from thefts committed by their dusky neighbors; but, as previously remarked, with a few exceptions, no white person's blood was shed in this valley by them, and their attacks were generally provoked, as in one or two cases which will be mentioned.

An attack upon some of the whites was at one time occasioned by a man by the name of Harris, who ordered the Indian, Big Rascal, out of the men's sleeping quarters, and who, upon the refusal of the savage to comply with the demand, resorted to the use of fists and boots, to make the order more forcible. Not long after the expulsion of Big Rascal, as narrated, the whites were alarmed by the Indian war-cry, and a party of Chippewas, headed by Masonaquet, a chief, was seen approaching. It was not a very pleasant sight,—the Indians coming, swinging their tomahawks and crying for blood, followed by their squaws, who, with their dismal wails were begging them to desist. But Mr Bullard, with a remarkable forethought, went out to meet the chief. "If you want blood," he said, "take mine first." Masonaquet paused in amazement, which allowed Mr. Bullard time to explain the matter. Upon hearing the whole truth, the chief admitted that Big Rascal was in the blame, and expressed himself willing to resume the friendly relations which had previously existed. It is quite possible that this daring act prevented much bloodshed, if not a general massacre.

In 1848, one George Wilson (no relation to Capt. Wilson) bought, hired or bribed a squaw, known as Mary Dirty-face, to marry him, Indian fashion. But the union did not prove a happy one. Mary Dirty-face, after the manner of some of the women now-a-days, absolutely refused to share her bed and board with her lord; and to retaliate, he siezed upon the goods with which he had bought or bribed her, and burned them. Not yet satisfied with his revenge, he purchased a gallon of whisky and a quantity of ipecac, and invited the Indians to have a big drunk with him, being careful, however, to drink none of the drugged whisky himself. The deed aroused the ire of the savages, as well it might, and as soon as they were sufficiently recovered, they sounded the terrible war-cry and started in pursuit of vengeance. George Wilson was warned in time, and escaped, which did not contribute much toward healing the wounds that the Indians had received at his hands. They made terrible threats against the peace of the whites, but finally became quieted without resorting to bloodshed. Perhaps it is needless to add that thenceforth Mary Dirty-face was considered as lawfully divorced from her lord and master.

The Indians did not call the white settlers by their real names, but christened them, Indian fashion, with appropriate cognomens, by which they were known and familiarly spoken of by their own people, as well Capt. Wilson was "Chah-no," (big nose); T. B. Wilson was called "Chah-ness," (little nose); J H Knapp was known as "Nepos-ke," or the great sleeper; Elisha Brown, an early settler, and a logger, was "Wah-ba-no," (morning dawn); Levi Vance, a partner of Brown's, was "O-wist-we ah," (blacksmith), and Lorenzo Bullard had the outlandish cognomen of "Che-puck-wah-nin-ny," which means a cook. As the latter person kept the boarding-house, it was to him that the hungry natives oftenest came begging Upon one occasion, the Indian, Nain-ne-aun-gabe, familiarly known by the whites as Little Chief, and really the most honorable man in the Chippewa nation, (if Indians are possessed of any honor) called on Bullard for some food, and Bullard put a half bushel of fried cakes on the table, and told Little Chief to help himself. The hungry native devoured five or six, then, spreading his blanket on the table, deliberately emptied all of the cakes into it, and made off with them, giving a grunt of satisfaction as he passed through the door. Bullard, too suprised to stop his progress, looked after the chief with widely opened eyes, and ejaculated: "By John Rogers, who would have thought the d——d Indian would have gobbled them all?"

THE MAN WITH THE WHITE SHIRT ON

In the spring of 1847, James Wilson, a brother of Capt. Wilson, came, on a keel-boat, to some point on Chippewa River, and walked thence to the home of the Captain, passing on his journey the residence of the Gilberts, situated two miles distant It being a warm day, he had removed his coat to facilitate his walking, and thus disclosed to the wondering Gilberts the fact that he was a man who wore a white shirt. All unconscious, however, that he was a subject of wonderment, he continued on his way, and arrived, in the course of time, at his brother's place of residence, so completely fatigued that it was necessary for him to go to bed, in order to recruit his wasted energies. Mrs Bullard, being at the Wilson's at the time of his arrival, invited him to rest at her house, deeming it the more quiet of the two. The invitation was accepted. But the young man had scarcely ensconsed himself in the inviting bed, before Mrs Bullard was waited upon by the entire Gilbert family, which consisted of four women and one man. There were two rooms in Bullard's cabin, one of which was used for a sleeping room; and after closing the door between the apartments, that the weary traveler might not be disturbed, Mrs Bullard sat down to entertain the party of callers. She had often invited the Gilbert family to make her a visit,—coming all together, instead of one at a time, as they were in the habit of doing; and now she expressed her surprise and pleasure at their being able to do so. "La!" returned Mrs Gilbert, fanning herself vigorously with her sun-bonnet, "we didn't come visiting. Bless you, we havn't time for that. The truth is, we saw a man pass our house with a biled shirt on, and we jist started after him full chase, to see what he is here for. A man must be a fool, or crazy, or something, to wear a biled shirt up here. Where is he, Mrs. Bullard? Is he here?" The lady, interrogated, informed the Gilberts of the fact that the stranger was at the time resting in one of her beds. "What's he want, and what's he doing here?" they all demanded in chorus. Without replying, Mrs Bullard stepped to the door, leading to the other apartment, and said to the traveler "Mr Wilson, you are waited upon by a deputation of ladies who are alarmed for the safety of any man that is reckless enough to wear a a white shirt. You will therefore please come out and give on account of yourself and of your business here." It is perhaps needless to add that the gentleman complied with the request, and ended his explanations by promising never to wear a white shirt again; and that the party returned home satisfied that his ignorance excused his offence. John H. Knapp, Esq., when at the mills, was more careful. He laid aside his dress clothes for the more popular ones of the backwoods men. Upon one occasion he substituted a pair of moccasins for his fine boots; but when he again needed the latter, he found one of them gone. Not wishing to appear upon the borders of civilization dressed like an Indian, he instituted a search for the missing article. He went to one wigwam and enquired about it. The occupants assured him that they did not steal, but they were sure their next neighbors did. The next neighbors told a similar story. Finally he entered a wigwam where he found an Indian lying on the ground, covered up with a blanket. He at once concluded that that Indian had his boot, and on snatching off the blanket he found that his conclusion was light, for, upon the soles of the old chap's moccasins, he discovered his boot top. He also, upon searching the wigwam, found the sole of the boot. But the Indian denied stealing the boot, and pretended not to know where he got it. Mr. Knapp retaliated by seizing a shot-gun, and taking it away with him to his quarters He was followed by a crowd of whooping savages, who, however, did not have courage to attack him, though they complained loudly about his treatment He very quietly informed them that his boots had cost as much as the gun, and that he intended to keep the latter in payment for what they had stolen "But we stole only one boot, and you take pay for both!" they exclaimed Finding Mr. Knapp determined to keep the gun, they dispersed; but they never could see the justice of paying for two boots when they had taken only one.

The amusements of the early settlers were dancing, card-playing, hunting and fishing; in the latter of which the women were often as expert as the men; and so great was the love of dancing, that parties have been known to go from Eau Claire to Chippewa Falls, breaking the way through deep snow, to attend a dance The fiddle was about all the kind of musical instrument known for many 'years The first piano was brought by Phineas Branch and wife, in 1855, to the company's hotel, then kept by Mrs. Bullard. While keeping the hotel, which she did during the absence of her husband who was in California, Mrs. Bullard received an offer of marriage from an old Indian chief, who admired her and pitied her lonely condition The hotel was destroyed by fire in 1859, and proved to be a great loss to the traveling public, and to the seekers of amusement who had made it their headquarters for many years. It was also in this hotel that the live men of what is now Dunn County, resolved no longer to countenance the evils of drunkeness and gambling by the sale of liquor, or by indulging in the amusement of card-playing. This occurred in 1854. A party had gathered one evening in the hotel bar-room to play for amusement. But they played for oysters, wine and finally money; and the whole resulted in something which they had not played for, viz, a quarrel, or row of some kind The unlooked-for result of that one evening's amusement set them to thinking, and being truly thinking men, they saw their error, and resolved thenceforth to make amends for it.

Previous to this, however, and as early as 1848, the Company had given up the liquor traffic It occurred in this wise Several rafts had been broken up and scattered about, through the inefficiency of drunken workmen, whereupon Capt. Wilson remarked rather snappishly that the miserable whisky was to blame for the whole thing "Why do you let them have it?" asked Mr Knapp "You bring it up," retorted the Captain "Yes, but you put it in your bills of needed supplies" "Well, next time you bring supplies, just leave it out," said Capt. Wilson Mr Knapp took the Captain at his word, and the next boat brought no liquor The men, who had been anxiously awaiting the arrival of a supply of their favorite beverage, glanced at the boat's freight, and finding none there, began to look black. "He has not brought a drop of whisky," they complained to the Captain. "How is this, Knapp?" asked that individual tersely, for the men's looks threatened mutiny "Where's the whisky?" "I forgot it," replied Knapp, and his interrogator knew what that meant "They will have to wait until the next time I go for supplies" It is needless to add that Mr Knapp ever after continued to forget that particular article, and that the men's bills no longer read as one of the old-time topers says his did, which was as follows

1847	*Blank Blankerson,*				*Dr*	
Jan 1,	To ——					6¼
" "	"	——	——	——	——	25
" "	"	——	——	——	——	12½
" "	"	——	——	——	——	25
Jan 2,	"	——	——	——	——	25
" "	"	——	——	——	——	25
" "	"	——	——	——	——	25
	To Sundries				1	43¾

Other parties, however, were willing to furnish liquor to all who could pay for it, and the liquor traffic was, therefore, not abolished except by the Company.

It was early in the spring of 1848, that the first steamboat came up the Chippewa River. The "Dr Franklin," of Galena, was bound for the upper Mississippi Mr Knapp was on board, having with him a crew of workmen and considerable freight He also had freight on a second boat, the "Highland Mary" It was found that Lake Pepin was blocked with ice. As the boats could not proceed on their regular trips, Mr. Knapp chartered the "Dr Franklin" to bring his men and freight to their destination, he, himself, becoming the pilot for the time He brought the steamboat safely through, and landed the men and freight at the mouth of the Red Cedar River. This started the subject of the possibility of navigating the Chippewa, and the " Dr. Franklin " was, in course of time, followed by a boat owned by H. S. Allen.

GOING A VISITING IN EARLY DAYS.

The houses of the early settlers were log cabins, containing not more than one or two rooms, and, in most cases, supplied with home-made furniture, barely sufficient to meet the wants of the inmates. A spare bed was a luxury which few, if any, had; and, when people went a visiting. it was as necessary for them to carry their beds with them as it was to take their clothing. Mr. Bullard tells of how he was once visited by a party during his residence on Hay River; and a description of the arrangements for sleeping is quite amusing. The party consisted of Capt. Wilson and wife, Oliver Gilbert and wife (now of Brownsville, Minn.) and B. Heard and wife. As usual, they all brought their beds with them. But the cabin was small, and could not afford room on the floor for three seperate beds; so one large bed was made up, and Mr. Bullard had to puzzle his wits to arrange the party in them so that one man would not be placed by the side of another man's wife. This is the way he arranged them, and it proved perfectly satisfactory to all:

Capt. Wilson.	Mrs. Wilson.	Mrs. Gilbert.	Oliver Gilbert.	B. Herd.	Mrs. Herd.

Mr. Bullard was always considered a good floor manager. Another description of some sleeping arrangements is still more comical. The Bullards were living at the lower mill in a cabin, with two rooms in it, each having a single door which opened outside. Another Gilbert family were the visitors this time. The Bullards had only two beds, and both in one room. One of these was usually occupied by Mr. and Mrs. Bullard, and the other by the two children, then little shavers, To arrange for Mr. and Mrs. Gilbert, who had not brought beds along, Mrs. Bullard decided to have Eugene sleep with her and her husband, and to put her daughter on a lounge, thus giving up one bed to the visitors Now it happened that Mrs. Gilbert was suffering with sick head-ache, and in consequence retired before dark. After dark, but before bed time, Mr. Bullard complained of being tired, and asked where he was to sleep His wife answered, "In our bed with Eugene." He misunderstood her to say, "In Eugene's bed." He went into the room, purposely without a light, and got into the children's bed The lady, supposing him to be her husband, did not speak. She noticed that he nudged her rather roughly with his elbow, but her head ached so hard that she crept off to the far side, and made no complaint After a while Mr. Gilbert asked to be shown to bed, and Mrs. Bullard, taking a light, led him to the chamber, where they found the pair asleep, and apparently totally unconscious of their close proximity to each other The consternation of all parties cannot be described Bullard's greatest trouble, however, was in getting to his own bed. His wife says that when he did go, he bore a flag of truce along with him

Mr. Bullard seems to have given people other causes to laugh at his expense several times The writer heard of a funny joke which was played on him, and will give it here. When or where it happened, it matters not Himself and wife were in a house where several young folks were visiting, and where the subject of spiritualism was being discussed, Mr Bullard disclaiming all belief in that theory. The young folks, assisted by Mrs Bullard, resolved to make him a believer, and as they could not command the spirits, they invented a mechanical contrivance to act in place It was an arrangement for making raps on the head-board of his bed, and was managed by a person in another room, by means of a wire running under the carpets Upon the night in question, Mr. Bullard retired after a stirring controversy upon spiritualism ; but Mrs Bullard lingered, for obvious reasons, a little longer than usual with the young folks When finally she sought her companion, she found him perched up in bed, on one elbow, listening with breathless attention "What is the matter ?" she asked "I have heard raps here !" he replied. "All imagination," she returned, with a toss of her head. "You have talked against spiritualism until you have made yourself believe it" But even while she spoke, three distinct raps were heard. "There!"" he exclaimed "Sure enough, you have got the raps after you ! Ask it to rap twice if you are a medium." "Please rap twice if I am a medium," said Mr Bullard, with terrible earnestness. The answer came, one, two. "Perhaps it is your father. Ask it." Slowly and solemnly the

33

victim put the question: "If you are my father, please rap twice." Again the answer came, one, two. Mrs Bullard began to edge toward the door. "Where are you going?" he inquired. "Going to find other quarters," she replied. "And leave me here alone?" "Yes, if you are a medium I am not going to live with you I won't live with a medium" "But I can't help it," he said piteously "I don't want to be a medium. Please don't go!" "Well, ask your spirit if it will stop rapping if I come to bed!" In a very anxious and solemn manner, Mr. Bullard asked "Father, will you stop rapping if my wife comes to bed?" One, two, the raps answered. Mrs. Bullard went to bed, and no more raps were heard; but the poor man tossed about all night, wondering how she could sleep so quietly while he was so restless. The next morning he looked so woe-begone that the young folks took pity on him, and informed him that it was all a joke But he was not angry at all. He was only too glad that it was not a reality, and that he was not a medium

Returning to the early times, tradition gives us a little anecdote, which shows how the people spent Sundays. It was one summer, at plumming time. Mr Bullard had worked hard all the week previous, and was very tired; still he did not fail to make one of a plumming party that started out on Sunday morning. Mr. and Mrs Ball, one of the Company, Mrs. Clair and Eugene Bullard, then a small boy, were the other members of the party. They went up the river in a canoe, the rowing, or rather poling, being done by the men, who could not agree as to the best method of performing that kind of work One of them found considerable fault with Mr. Bullard, who became a little angry thereat—all the more so because he was heated and tired with the exertion. The consequence was, that when the canoe was landed near the thicket, Mr. Bullard threw Eugene across his shoulders and started for home on foot. Arriving there, he shook the boy off, and, straightening himself up, exclaimed: "Well, if Jesus Christ reigns another Sunday, I'll REST." It is needless to add that Sunday service was not held in this part of the county at that time.

THE FIRST MARRIAGES

The first marriage in this part of the country, was in 1847. The parties were a Mr. Whitcomb and Mrs. Clair. The Circuit Justice of the Peace, J. W. Bass, happened to be at Chippewa Falls and he came, over and performed the ceremony. The marriage took place at the Company's kitchen, and Mrs. Wilson provided the supper But it happened that when the second couple, Margaret Scott and Thomas

Piercewell, wished to be united, there was no one near who had power to tie the knot. This difficulty was obviated by a marriage contract, which was drawn up and signed in presence of witnesses. After the signing was over, the parties invited their friends to the wedding feast, which consisted of pork and beans, and whisky, which were the staple articles of food at that time. A dance ended the festivities. This singular marriage occurred in 1850, and proved satisfactory to both parties.

FIRST DEATH AND BURIAL OF A WHITE WOMAN

The first death of a white woman in this section of country, also occurred in 1850. Mrs. Fannie Vale, probably the first woman who was a resident here, was the victim. She had lived a hard life, and, in the matter of civilization, she was but little in advance of her companions, the savages. Her husband, John Vale, was a rough, uneducated old man, and withal much given to drink. After the old woman had become ill, she was taken to the residence of one A. Lemon, whose wife was an Indian medicine-woman, that she might have the benefit of Mrs. Lemon's skill. One winter day, the tipsy John informed Mrs. Bullard, in his profane way, that Fannie was dying. Mrs. Bullard did not believe the statement, but she immediately set out for Lemon's cabin, two miles distant, to ascertain whether or not it was true. She found the poor creature lying upon the floor, upon some rags and skins, half naked and already in the agonies of death. The look of blank amazement, that spread over the lady's face, convinced John that the visitor understood the exact situation, and nudging her with his elbow, he exclaimed "You did not believe me when I told you that it was as true as h—l she was a dying." Then he dropped to the floor to the side of his wife, and, twisting a lock of her gray hair about his fingers, much as if he was about to scalp her, he produced a dull jack-knife, and tried to cut off the lock of hair, greatly to the annoyance of the sick woman, who writhed under the infliction. "What are you doing, John?" asked Mrs. Bullard, rushing to the rescue. "I'm going to have a lock of her hair, it's all I ever 'spect to have of her now," he replied. Mrs. Bullard begged him to desist, promising that she would see that a lock of his wife's hair should be saved for him. This satisfied him, and crawling behind the stove, he soon fell into a drunken sleep, leaving his visitor and the squaw to attend to the dying woman, who passed eternityward sometime in the evening. Mrs. Bullard sent home for some of her own clothes, in which to lay out the destitute creature's body. A board was procured, but there were no tables or chairs to hold the corpse, and the best that they could do was to place it on a couple of barrels, which held the winter's supply of pork and venison. When night came on, the Lemon family crawled into the one bed that the cabin contained, and Mrs Bullard was left to keep the dreary watch alone. About midnight John Vale awoke from his drunken sleep, and getting up upon his haunches, like an animal, began to sing "Good-bye, Molly" Mrs Bullard tried to hush him by asking if he knew that Fannie was dead. He replied with an oath that he knew it too well. Presently he got up, and, going to the side of the corpse, uncovered the face and looked long and earnestly at it. Finally he turned and faced the visitor with the remark · "God thinks he's done it, I 'spose He might have took me as well as her, and I am going to drown myself I'll be even with Him." Mrs. Bullard, knowing that the supply store would sell him no more whisky until after the funeral, did not try to detain him. She knew that it was whisky, not death, of which he was in search. The long, terrible night was ended, at last. The Lemon's arose and began preparations for breakfast. They swung the corpse one way, and took a piece of venison from one barrel; then they swung it the other way and fished a bit of pork out of the other barrel ; then the body was placed in its proper position, and left there until the time of the funeral. The only mode of travel was by trains —narrow one-horse sleighs, roughly constructed by the back-woods-men themselves. Three of these constituted the funeral equipage A rough box answered for a coffin, and in order to carry it, the end board of one of the trains had to be removed. When all was ready for a start, some men had to ride on the train to hold the coffin on. The remainder of the people who had come to attend the funeral, viz. a few workmen and squaws, took seats on the other trains; and the funeral procession moved on. Up to this time, John had not made his appearance. In fact, nobody missed him, or cared where he was. Everybody in those days considered it his business to help bury or marry a neighbor, regardless of his or her religion, politics or social position. Then, knowing John's failings, no one took the trouble to hunt him up, and ask for instructions from him. It was a bright, winter morning. The snow was knee-deep where it was unbroken, and it was covered by a crust that made traveling irksome. The burial ground was about two miles and a half distant from Lemon's cabin, and was on the top of quite a steep hill Up this hill the drivers found it impossible to draw the loaded trains, since the crusted

snow was in this place unbroken. In consequence, the people all
got out, the men going ahead of the train that carried the corpse, and
the women waiting in the deep snow to consider whether or not it
would be best to accompany the corpse to the grave. This left the
coffin unheld and liable to slide off, unless great care was observed
But the horse of this single train found it no easy task to ascend the
hill, and the driver was obliged most vigorously to apply the whip in
order to start the animal at all. The result of such treatment was a
sudden jerk that shook the coffin off, and as box, corpse and all went
rolling down the hill, John Vale appeared suddenly upon the scene.
Seeing that the driver was evidently unconscious of the accident, the
bereaved husband began helloong, gesturing and slapping his hands
together in the wildest and most absurd manner. "Stop' stop' stop'
I say. D—n you, don't you know you've left Fanny behind' You've
left Fannie, I say!" The scene can be better imagined than described. The one white woman who witnessed it stood knee-deep in
the snow, and, solemn as the occasion was, smiled visibly at the lu-
dicrous picture. John succeeded finally in attracting the driver's
attention. Then it being found impossible to draw the corpse up the
steep hill on the train, the men clambered up, bearing it on their
shoulders, and hid it from view by a shallow covering of frozen earth
and snow. John, as well as Fannie, is now among the things that
were, but the survivors who attended that funeral will never cease to
recall with a smile the first burial of a white woman in Dunn County

THE FIRST RESIDENT PREACHER

Some time about the year 1854, a school house was erected, and,
it having become necessary to engage a teacher, the energetic Captain Wilson conceived the idea of advertising for a person who would
teach school and also conduct religious exercises. The advertise-
ment was answered by a bashful bachelor, the Rev. Joshua Pittman,
who was somewhat "set back" when he learned that he was to
"preach Sundays, teach school week-days, and pack shingles nights"
He, however, engaged, and continued his labors until 1859, when a
regular district school was organized

As a consequence of going to meeting on Sundays, the women
began to long for more fashionable apparel than they had hitherto
worn. But so intense was the general sentiment against all kinds of
finery, that no one was brave enough to cast off the sun-bonnet for
the dress bonnet of the outside world, until the advent of Mrs G. M.
Fowler, who appeared in church one Sabbath with the then fashion-

able relation of the "sky-scraper" on her head. The bonnet, and not the sermon, was the center of attraction that day. Little billets of comment were passed around in the audience; and, though few could have told what the sermon was about, all could give the exact dimensions and make-up of the first dress bonnet ever worn in Menomonie.

In March, 1856, the county of Dunn was organized, with a small hamlet, known as Dunnville, for the county seat. It was named in honor of Judge Dunn, first judge of the district. But the village of Menomonie was laid out in 1859, and a vote of the people the same year, removed the county seat to the latter place. The first term of Circuit Court was held in September, 1857, the resident lawyers being E. B. Bundy and C. S. Bundy, the former of whom is still practicing law in Menomonie.

But though Dunn county was organized in 1856, the majority of the United States lands did not come into market until 1860. The Fox River Improvement Company having received a munificent grant of land, in view of services to be rendered, by which a choice of government lands was given them, had claimed a much larger portion than was their due. In 1860, their claim was adjusted. They chose the best lands west of the Red Cedar river, and gave up the lands on the east side, to the government. The government lands were immediately put into market, and were bought by substantial people, who soon surrounded themselves with all the comforts which farmers usually have.

NEWSPAPER HISTORY

Dunn county is indebted to Knapp, Stout & Co., for an early introduction of a newspaper press. The "Dunn County Lumberman" was started in April, 1860, with C S. Bundy, a young lawyer of considerable ability, as editor. Upon the outbreak of the rebellion, the young editor exchanged the pen for the sword, and his brother, E. B. Bundy, an able lawyer, became editor. The third editor in order of time, was Thomas Phillips, a Democrat of some ability, the paper meanwhile supporting the Republican party. In 1865, the concern was purchased by Dr. Benjamin. During this administration Charles Mears, now of the "Polk County (Minn) Press," bought a half interest in the printing office, and upon his advent, April 7th, 1866, the paper changed its name to the "Dunn County News" Early in September of the same year, we find Mears' name withdrawn without even a good bye, and Dr Benjamin's continued alone.

A year later, Wilson & Messenger bought out Dr Benjamin, and S. W. Hunt took the editorial chair. This firm enlarged the paper and otherwise improved it The next change was a sale to Flint & Weber the present proprietors, about 1871 These men show a degree of enterprise in the management of the "News," manifested by only a few proprietors of county newspapers Their large, well-filled sheet is printed entirely at home, and its "insides" have never become so weak as to need patent ones Unlike many of its cotemporaries, the "Dunn County News" of 1875, will not cause the casual reader to undervalue the place which it represents

Outside the line above sketched were a couple of newspaperial spasms or episodes, which deserve notice in this connection Anti-monopolistic feelings had become sufficiently warm to call for a new paper, about the year of grace, 1871, and Rev. E Thompson brought in the "People's Press." Its career was about equally brilliant and brief—it lived seven weeks on "faith alone," and expired Next came the "Lean Wolf," by Van Waters, an old editor of no mean ability, but his "Lean Wolf" died of chronic leanness

The moral deducible from these reformatory spasms may be this: It is abundantly benevolent to make two blades of grass grow where only one grew before, but it is not always practicable in newspaperdom

WAR TIMES—HEROIC WOMEN

When the war of the rebellion began, some of the women of Menomonie proved themselves heroic, indeed. The village was new and small, and the families settled there did not feel able to endure more hardships than were already theirs Men were disposed to shrink from what they knew to be their duty, because to go to war was to leave their wives and children, mothers and sisters, to battle with the hardships alone. Some women, too, were faint-hearted, and clung to their protectors, faint and weeping, whenever the latter showed a disposition to answer the nation's call At this stage of affairs, a few heroic women inspired every soul with patriotism, by their voices and their example. Miss Eliza Wilson, a young girl, daughter of Captain Wilson, arose in a war meeting, and expressed herself willing to accompany any company that would organize, to share with its members the hardships of the march, and to nurse them if they fell ill, or were wounded, a resolution which she actually carried into effect Mrs. Bullard made several stirring speeches, which nerved the faint-hearted to action One of these speeches, we copy from a "Lumberman " of that date. Only a portion of a company had been organized, and the heroic women were working to fill the ranks. There had just been a war meeting, and speaking of that, the "Lumberman" says:

"After the meeting adjourned, the company formed in line and marched to the tune of Yankee Doodle through the principal streets and serenaded some of our citizens; among others, L Bullard, Esq , who responded in his usual happy manner Mrs. Bullard also came forward and said · " Soldiers, I regret that I have but one son to give to my country, he is a mere stripling, but the good book tells us that · 'The battle is not to the strong, nor the race to the swift, but to him that endureth to the end.' Soldiers, I place him in your keeping, hoping and trusting that you will cling together like a band of brothers. You have taken your lives in your hands to go forth in defense of your county, and I hope that as long as there is a man left, you will not suffer our national flag to be dishonored You leave behind you, friends who will watch your course, and if, as I am sure you will, you fight valiantly in the cause of your country, you will merit and receive their warmest gratitude and the plaudits of your friends and countrymen. If you lack one man, Mr Bullard shall go too.' "

Such heroism could not fail to bring forth a response , and when Captain Wilson and his wife declared that they would own no son who shrank from going to the assistance of his country, the lagging ones stepped forward and were enrolled

The first company ever raised in Chippewa Valley was the Dunn County Pinery Rifles, afterwards Company K of the Fifth Wisconsin Its officers were Capt. William Evans, Lieutenant C. R. Bayard and Lieutenant J A Hill It was mustered into service July 13th, 1861, by Captain McIntire, of the regular army. The officer in command was Col Amasa Cobb. The regiment was accompanied to the field by Miss Eliza Wilson. The regiment was in several engagements, and won honors which secured for it the commendation of General McClellan At the battle of Golden Farm, Virginia, Capt Evans was mortally wounded His death occurred August 1st, 1862. The regiment had fared ill. Disease and the shots of the enemy had laid many of the soldiers low, and Company K had only a handful of men left, when a second company from Dunn County, headed by Captain J. M Mott, reported ready for action. This new company took the place of the unfortunate one, and also became Company K of the Fifth Wisconsin Infantry Captain Mott became so exhausted at the battle of Gettysburg that he was left on the march, and afterwards sent to Frederick City, Maryland, where he died, July 26th, 1863

He was succeeded in command by Capt Henry C Farwell We can mention only a few of the brave men who went in the two companies from Dunn County Henry H Stout, at the time of his death second lieutenant of Company K, was a young man of great promise Free from all bad habits, pure hearted and brave, he had won the love and respect of all who knew him He was killed in the action of Spottsylvania Court House, May 10th, 1864 His death to this day is remembered with deep regret Henry C Farwell, promoted as first lieutenant May 14th, 1863, was wounded November 7th, 1863, in the action of Brandy Station, Virginia Of the officers who passed safely through, we note the names of James Deerey, Thomas Blan, Julius A Hill, T S West, C S Bundy, M H Wilson and M W. Heller

HIGH WATER

Before closing the early history of Menomonie, the writer wishes to mention the high water freshets, which have occurred at different periods. On the 12th of June, 1839, the water was higher in both the Chippewa and Red Cedar rivers, than it has been since, or was known to be before that time, by the oldest settler, either white man or Indian At that time the water overflowed all the bottom lands, and at the Dalles of the Chippewa it was eighteen feet above the ordinary height of the river The few people who were then living on the Red Cedar and the Chippewa, were frightened, and thought that Lake Superior had broken through to the head waters of those streams, and was empting itself into the Mississippi by those outlets. In 1846, the water was again very high in the Mississippi, and in 1847 the water in the Chippewa and Red Cedar was so very high that the logs of H S. Allen & Co's boom at Chippewa Falls, broke loose and went adrift. The last high water of note was in 1859, which was a very disastrous year for lumbermen, as lumber sold as low as from six dollars to eight dollars and fifty cents per thousand feet

DUNN COUNTY IN 1873

Dunn County contains twenty-four townships, and an area of 552,960 acres. The eastern portion consists of prairie lands; the western is rolling, and covered by immense forests The Chippewa river waters the southeast part; the Eau Galla the southwest; while the Red Cedar runs through from north to south. These streams and their tributaries furnish numerous good mill powers. Hard woods and sandstone and limestone abound The chief manufacturing interest is lumbering. About 80,000,000 feet of lumber are manufac-

34

tured annually. The county is crossed from east to west by the West Wisconsin Railway, bringing it into direct connection with the outside world.

The present village of Menomonie consists of a population of about three thousand five hundred people, and is one of the most picturesque of inland towns. The dam on which Knapp, Stout & Co.s mammoth saw and grist mills are situated, forms a lake a mile and a half long by over three-fourths of a mile wide. This lake is bounded on the east by picturesque bluffs or points of land, upon one of which, a mile from the village, is located the beautiful cemetery, recently laid out and platted by those widely and favorably known landscape architects, Cleveland & French, of Chicago. On the southwest of this lake, on high ground, is situated the residence of Mr. Andrew Tainter, which rivals in elegance any of the suburban villas of the large eastern cities. A little to the north of Mr. Tainter's grounds, is Captain Wilson's hospitable and comfortable mansion. At the outlet of this lake is built a large and substantial dam, of unique construction with numerous gates and chute. Near this dam, and on the west or right bank of the river, are located the different and numerous buildings, stores, warehouses, machine shop, foundry, blacksmith and wagon shops, boarding houses, dwelling and tenant houses, etc., etc, necessary to carry on the great business of this Lumbering Company. Here also Wilson Creek empties its waters into this great reservoir, a few rods above the dam, on the main Red Cedar river. This creek is a beautiful and romantic stream, bordered with high, rocky bluffs, it abounds in speckled trout. Its rapid current is stayed near its outlet by the construction of a dam, which supplies the power to run the Company's shingle and planing mills.

After passing out of the lake or mill pond, the Red Cedar (called by the citizens the "Menomonie River") again assumes its natural size, and with a rapid current runs over a rocky bed, in a westerly course, one fourth of a mile, and then turns southward. On a high plateau on the northwest, or right bank of this rapid stream, in a picturesque and romantic spot among the pines, and overlooking the river, is the residence of Mr J. H. Knapp. One of the partners of the firm of Knapp, Stout & Co, Mr. T. B. Wilson, formerly of Reeds Landing, Minnesota, has lately taken up his residence in Menomonie, and has built a house on the village side, attractive in style and pleasantly situated, and which adds to the good appearance of the town.

The village side of the river has many recent settlers, some of whom are doing a business which rivals, in some of its branches, the famous company on the other side; and this side, with its stores, churches, court-house, school-houses, printing office and dwellings, constitute the village proper. The native trees, on both sides, have, in many places, been left standing, and lend much of the pictur- esque to the appearance of the village.

There are several public buildings here worthy of note. The court house, built in 1871, is a brick structure, with dressed stone trimmings, and cost forty-five thousand dollars. Canute Thompson was the contractor, and his work is proof sufficient of his superior ability. The public school building, erected in 1869, is one of the best in this part of the state, and was built at an expense of nearly twenty thousand dollars. In 1873, school district number one built a second school-house in Coddington's addition, at a cost of five thou- sand dollars. During the winter of 1872, the county jail, a wooden structure, was burned, and in 1874, a new brick building, for the same purpose, was built under contract, by Ole Olson, for ten thousand dollars. The Baptists have two churches. The first of these was built and furnished by Captain Wilson. It is frescoed, upholstered with rep, lighted with gas, and furnished with an expensive organ. Besides these there are several other tasty churches. The only thing in the line of public buildings, which Menomonie seems to lack, is a first-class hotel. There are three or four good hotel buildings here, but none of them are conducted in a manner in keeping with the en- terprise of the village. The Menomonie House, kept by C. H. Mc- Cabe, is said to be the best of the three. It belongs to Knapp, Stout & Co., and is for sale.

Menomonie has also a Reading Room. Some of the enterprising ladies, with a view toward keeping the young men from saloons, clubbed together and opened an establishment where the young folks could spend their evenings. They intend to have, in addition to the reading room, a refreshment room. This is a highly praise-worthy institution, and if every community would establish such in its midst, the saloons would in time have to close for lack of custom. Mrs. M. L. Mott, widow of the lamented Capt. M. L. Mott, is the librarian of the Menomonie Reading Room.

Though the citizens, on both sides of the river, unite in establishing good institutions, there seems to be a feeling of rivalry existing be- tween the two sides of the river, or rather between many of the business men of Menomonie proper and Knapp, Stout & Co. The company, like all powerful organizations, is called a monopoly, and as such is frequently fought at elections, town meetings, etc ; and it often, though not always, wins the victory The sensitive, claim quite truly, that Menomonie is a flourishing village in itself, independent of the company that started it into life. But for all this, it cannot be denied, by the unbiased, that the Company is the great motive power of the community, as it furnishes employment for hundreds of men, while its wealth is constantly enriching and adding to the beauty of the village.

Menomonie was originally platted by Knapp, Stout & Co I Coddington made an addition to the village, in 1865, of thirty-two blocks. The lots in this addition, at first sold at twenty-five dollars each. They now bring three hundred dollars and upward. Martin H. Wilson and Mrs. E Morgan, have also made additions to Menomonie

Several smart villages beside Menomonie have sprung up in Dunn county One of these is Dunnville, situated near the mouth of Red Cedar river, twelve miles south of Menomonie It was settled in 1850. A man named Lamb was the first settler. Amos Colburn kept the first hotel in Dunville. John McCauley took up his residence then in 1853 A large portion of Dunville is owned by Knapp, Stout & Co.

Eau Galla, located in the southwest part of the hard woods, is a thriving little village on the Eau Galla river. It, like most other places in Dunn county, is the center of a lumbering district. The first mill at Eau Galla was built in 1840, under the direction of Savage, Wales & Co. This firm sold to Carson & Eaton in 1844, who built a large steam mill in 1852, which had the misfortune of being burned in 1862. A mill with three gang saws was erected and running the next year. Later, Eaton sold out his interest in the property to E. D. Rand, of Burlington, and the firm has since been Carson & Rand. This company also have a large flouring mill at Eau Galla

A mill was built at Cedar Falls in 1859, by Burry & McCormick. Later, it passed into the hands of Maxwell, McGilton & Co., who owned it until a few years ago, when Jewett & Son bought it at Sheriff's sale Quite a little village is springing up at this point

The Downsville mill was built in 1860 by Capt. Downs, on a site where Ebenezer Thompson had attempted to build a mill a few years before, but failed on account of a freshet which destroyed his work and impoverished him The mill was bought by Knapp, Stout & Co , who enlarged and improved it.   Here is also a little village, which is steadily improving   Downsville is situated on the Red Cedar river, eight miles south of Menomonie.

THE LIQUOR WAR

In the year 1874, a few of the go-ahead women of Menomonie resolved to put a stop to the liquor traffic, and their influence at the polls was such that a law, forbidding its sale, was passed   The practicability of such a law in a single town is questioned by many, but having caused its adoption, the women were determined that those who broke it should be punished.   It was like one man fighting an army, but women who could show such heroism when their country was needing aid, would not be likely to falter themselves, or fail to instill in their daughters' minds some of their own heroism, at a time when the law was being transgressed   A caustic old settler, in a note, says.

"The last great social spasm in Menomonie was the anti-liquor vote of last spring; and the anties, or, as some wags put it, the "aunties," carried the day.   The ladies are now prosecuting the saloon-men, with unflagging zeal, and average success.   But the end is not yet.   The coming election promises to be ardent, spirits or no spirits."

Since the commencement of the liquor war of this place, the vexed problem of whether or not lager-beer is intoxicating, has been decided in the negative.   A brewer was arrested for selling a keg of beer to one of the citizens.   He was fined, but appealed his case to a higher court   Great excitement prevailed when it was brought before Judge Humphrey.   Several men swore that beer can intoxicate, and several men that it can not   The judge seemed to be slightly prejudiced in favor of the beer, for he demanded to know of the temperance men how they knew beer to be intoxicating, and if it had ever intoxicated them   They, of course, did not like to own to such a weakness, and cited what they had seen.   But he waived such evidence, telling them that they must be able to speak from experience or not at all   He said, moreover, that he had nothing to do with any beer except the contents of that particular keg in question, which had been seized and brought to court as evidence.   What he wished to decide was whether that keg contained any intoxicating beverage   By an order given, the contents were tasted, but as it had been two days tapped, and the beer was really "flat," the decision was that that particular keg contained nothing that could intoxicate any one, and a verdict was rendered in accordance with the facts. Since then, it is said, the brewer pursues his regular vocation unmolested by the law.

Another case was equally as remarkable. While Justice Hull was in the act of fining a saloon-keeper for breaking the liquor law, a man fresh from the dentist's hands, came into Hull's drug store to get some whisky to rinse his bleeding mouth. A Mr Johnson, a school teacher, with no thought except to be kind, asked Justice Hull if he should get the desired article. Hull, whether thinking of the question or not, nodded assent; at least, so thought the questioner, and he poured a small amount into a glass. This was used for the purpose mentioned, after which the patient laid down a ten-cent script in payment, and Johnson put it into the money-drawer. The saloon-keeper who had been fined, saw the whole proceedings, and he immediately had the teacher arrested for selling liquor. Johnson called on Hull to witness his innocence; but, Hull disclaiming any knowledge of the affair, the former was fined ten dollars and costs for violating the liquor law. He will probably harden his heart in future when suffering humanity wants whisky, especially if he is in a town where no licenses are granted

SETTLERS OF MENOMONIE AND DUNN COUNTY

In a work like this, it is impossible to give an complete list of the settlers of the county, or even of the village of Menomonie. Only a few of the older and more prominent ones will be noticed in this article, and to each of these but a short space can be devoted, on account of lack of room

Jo Benson, an old man in the employment of Knapp, Stout & Co., has lived in Menomonie over forty years. He is the man who claims to have been in the expedition, said to have been under command of Jeff Davis, that visited this county at an early day.

Perry Curtis opened a farm in Dunn county, in 1846 It is situated near Eau Galla mill, and is owned in part by Carson & Eaton. Another farm was owned by Frank Ames and sons in 1847. They were among the first farmers in the county.

Mud Creek Valley, east of Menomonie, had B Fowler for its first settler This was in 1852 The Massey settlement commenced by the advent of H H Steves in 1856

Captain Moore laid out a farm of twenty-two hundred acres, about twelve miles up the Red Cedar, which he sold to Knapp, Stout & Co in 1865.

Sherburne Prairie, a little northeast of Menomonie, was laid out into farms by Sherburne & Harrington

D. B. Downs, now of Eau Claire, settled here soon after the arrival of the Bullards

Levi Vance, an Indian trader, now dead, visited this part of the country forty-seven years ago, and made his home here until called to another. He built the first hotel in Menomonie proper which he named the Vance House. This house, now called the Union House, is kept by his son-in-law, Peter Perrault at the present time

John Rogler, tinner, began working for the company in 1862. At the breaking out of the war he entered the army, and when the nation was again blessed with peace, he took up his tools a second time at the old place

Simon Marugg, general foreman of outside matters, for Knapp, Stout & Co., came to work for said company in 1851. He was the first soldier to enlist in Chippewa Valley, for the war of the rebellion and one of three who would not wait for a company to be raised be fore reporting himself ready for action. He was enrolled at Madison, as orderly sergeant of Company B of the Sixth Infantry, and was wounded at the battle of Gettysburg. In 1864, he was elected sheriff of Dunn county.

William Warren, blacksmith, has worked for Knapp, Stout & Co., the entire thirteen years of his residence in Menomonie

A. J. Depew has lived in Dunn county since 1855. He is a mill-wright, and has been in the employ of the company for over eleven years.

About the year 1857, William McKahin arrived in Menomonie with his family, consisting of himself, wife, three sons and four daughters. For a number of years, Mr. McKahin was employed by Knapp, Stout & Co., as head clerk in their store, it was through the influence of Mr. John H. Knapp that they left their many friends in Washington, Pennsylvania, and came to this place. While still employed by the Company, he purchased a tract of land six miles from Menomonie, and afterwards improved it, and made it his home for one year. But finding the work too laborious for a man of his advanced years, he left the farm came back to the village, and purchased a house, in which he resided at the time of his death. After leaving the farm he owned a livery stable, and for two years was proprietor of the Menomonie House. The disease of which he died was paralysis. He was confined to his room for two years previous to his death, which occurred October 10th, 1872

His estimable wife survived him but a few weeks. She died of apoplexy, November 27th 1872, in Minneapolis, Minnesota, where she had gone to spend the winter with her daughters, Mrs. Downs and Mrs. Newsom. Of Mr and Mrs McKahan's children, their three sons are living in the village. James B. is engaged in the mercantile business, and Samuel D. has been postmaster for the last four years, filling that office creditably to himself, and to the satisfaction of the people. The four daughters, Mrs. Downs, Mrs. Newson, Mrs Keith and Miss Sarah E. McKahan are in Minneapolis, Minnesota. J. B. McKahan was the first merchant on the east side of the river, and next to Knapp, Stout & Co., in order of time, in the town. He opened up in 1860, with a cash capital of one hundred and fifty-seven dollars, and a stock of one hundred and seventy-five dollars, owing on his first invoice eighteen dollars. His store was the first in the village proper, and the builders of this and several of the buildings which soon after followed, had to clear away the brush before laying the foundations. J B. McKahan carries a large stock of general merchandise, and is accounted one of the rich men of the village, although he was often taunted in the commencement by towns-people, who offered him ten dollars for his stock.

Dr. W. A. Burry, a noted optician, has had eighteen years experience in Dunn County. His residence is at Cedar Falls.

In 1858, G. M. Fowler, millwright and surveyor, visited Menomonie for the purpose of looking up a new location. While passing through the six-mile woods between this place and Lake Pepin on his way hither, he met a party of Sioux warriors, adorned with the scalps and trophies of a victory after a recent battle with the Chippewas. The sight was more curious than pleasant to a man who had known nothing of pioneer life. But he was pleased with the country and decided to settle in it, which he did during the next year. Mr. Fowler served as justice of the peace for three years, commencing in 1862, and was elected county surveyor in 1867, which position he filled for two years. Mrs G M. Fowler opened the first millinery store and the second store of any kind started in Menomonie proper, in the year 1862 in her own house. She is now doing business on Thirty-fourth street, and has on hand one of the largest and finest assortments of goods to be found in Chippewa Valley. She is also agent for the Victor sewing machine, and her sales in this branch of business alone have amounted to over $5,000 in two years time. The Fowlers have added to the growth of Menomonie by the erection of

three store building, a photograph gallery, and a fine private residence. The private residence, they gave up to the county officers, upon the removal of the county seat from Dunnville to this place. It was occupied by them three years, and until county buildings could be erected. William Fowler, the only surviving son of this enterprising family, is an accomplished musician, and, though only seventeen years old, is a thorough and successful teacher of the piano forte. He is also agent for the New England organ.

N. C Eytcheson began logging for Knapp, Stout & Co, twenty-five years ago, in company with the man Wickham, who was murdered by the Indians. Later, he bought a large farm, which he was unfortunate enough to lose in some kind of a speculation. He was the builder of the Menomonie House, which he run for sixteen months, and then sold to the Company. He is now a dealer in boots and shoes and groceries. (In the same store, the writer found an old woman who evidently deals largely in tongue, but judging from appearances we would not like to recommend the article.)

Jacob Miller, painter and artist, has been in Menomonie since 1856.

Dr E. G. Benjamin the first resident practitioner was among the first builders-up of the village proper, was owner and editor of the "Dunn County News" about two years, was appointed and afterwards elected County Judge, and filled other smaller offices

Samuel W Hunt, attorney at law, located in Menomonie in the month of March, 1866. He was District Attorney in 1867 and 1868, and member of the Assembly in 1868. He was also at one time editor of the "Dunn County News." He is still in Menomonie, engaged in the practice of law

S B French came to Dunn County in November, 1855, and for fourteen years following that time, was book-keeper for Knapp, Stout & Co. Of late years, he has been engaged in banking, real estate and merchandise. His store on Thirty fourth street offers one of the best assortment of goods to be found in Chippewa Valley. His wife was Virginia Bullard, daughter of Lorenzo Bullard, one of the first settlers of Menomonie

Theodore Neys, millwright and machinist, has worked seventeen years for Knapp, Stout & Co

W M Dunn, filer in the Company's mill, became a resident of the county in 1854

M. Halfhide has worked thirteen years for the Company.

B S. Thorne, wagon maker, claims seventeen years residence in this
35

part of the country, ten years of which he has been in the employ of the Company.

Frederick Bonnell, now largely engaged in photography, came to this village in 1869, from Eau Claire After putting up a gallery and finding it too small for the amount of work he had to do, he erected a building, two stories in height, on Thirty-fourth street. The whole of this large building is occupied as a gallery. The engraving in this book is from a photograph taken by him

George Tonnar, a German-American, emigrated from Dubuque in 1869, and settled here. He started in the drug business in November, 1871, on Thirty-fourth street, and he still reports trade in his line as brisk. He was elected in 1874 as Superintendent of Public Schools, and resigned on account of business pressure. He is now a Justice of the Peace, and between the men who will not obey the liquor law and the women who declare the law shall be obeyed, he has found his duties rather irksome.

J. B Sprague, proprietor of the Stage Line from Menomonie to Rice Lake, located at Menomonie in 1856.

H. S. Hull became a resident of Menomonie in 1865. He went into business as a druggist with Dr Pease, in a building now occupied by Hunt & Freeman, lawyers At the end of the year he bought out the doctor's interest. He is still in the business on Thirty-fourth street

E. J Newsom, assistant postmaster, has had but eighteen months residence in Menomonie He is now establishing a " Badger State Publishing Agency," which promises to be a complete success.

Frank E Pease, architect and builder, became a resident of Menomonie in 1861, and erected a drug store, which was the fourth building in the village proper. Dr. W. C Pease had his office there. Frank enlisted in 1863. At the close of the war he went to Michigan. In 1873, he returned to Menomonie, bringing his family with him He has the contract to build the Episcopal church

John Noulan, lumberman, has been in Menomonie since November, 1854

Dr. J. M Gates located in Menomonie in 1870. He reports a very chequered life. He married young, and was obliged to pursue his studies after he had a family. He graduated at Jefferson Medical College, only a short time previous to his coming to Menomonie; though he had treated chronic diseases for over fifteen years by medicine and magnetism combined. He is now writing a book, which he entitles "Physiobiethic Practice." He claims that a physician can simply assist nature by medicines—that drugs act either chemically, physiologically, alopathically, or homeopathically, and gives an illustration of the action of each. He also endeavors to show why small quantities of medicine, under certain conditions, produce marked and immediate results. The new theory is claimed to be based on the experiments made upon the nervous system by Brown, Dubois, Raymond and others. He aims to have the book gotten up in a manner that all may understand. It will quite likely meet with attention from all schools of practice.

F. J. McLean, attorney at law, began practice here in 1868.

P. C. Holmes, dealer in furniture, carpeting, etc., took up his residence here in 1860.

H. C. Blenis, contractor and builder, settled in Menomonie in 1871.

Dr. W. F. Nichols began practice in Menomonie in 1869, after having spent four years in the medical department of the army. He is erecting a building for the accommodation of patients requiring surgical treatment, his rapidly increasing practice having made such an institution necessary.

Thomas Condon, grocer on Thirty-fourth street, did not begin business here until 1874.

William Schultts and Albert Quilling, merchants on Main street, came to this place in 1855. They were poor boys, and worked as day laborers to lay the foundation of a prosperous business. They built the large store which they now occupy.

T. A. Goodman, proprietor Goodman's wagon and carriage shops, settled here in 1863.

R C Bierce, attorney at law, dates his time of settlement here from 1871.

G. Ordeman, proprietor of Ordeman's paint shop and store, located on Mud Creek eighteen years ago. Three years after, he came to Menomonie and engaged in his present business.

J. F. Edwards visited Menomonie in 1860. Six years later he became a permanent settler here, and started a sash, door and blind factory, which was burned in 1870 by an incendiary. In 1872, in company with his son, he engaged in the hardware business. The firm, known as Edwards & Son, has two large stores on Thirty-fourth street, and monopolizes the hardware business of Menomonie proper.

James Galloway and family settled here in 1854. He worked for Knapp, Stout & Co., about two years, then began farming near the village, at which business he still continues. He has two sons' George and William, the former of these is the village drayman, the latter is studying for the ministry.

T S Heller looked in on the Dunn county people in 1857, but did not become a permanent settler until 1860. Previous to the war, he kept the Tainter House at Dunnville. for a season He enlisted subsequently, and served in the army for over three years. Upon his return, he became landlord of the Menomonie House, and filled that position for a year. He is now engaged in the insurance business.

Joseph Brunk, proprietor of Brunk's Mills, four and a half miles from Menomonie, has been a resident of Dunn county for over eleven years.

George K. Irvine, for whom Irving's Creek was named, and formerly proprietor of Irvine's Mills, has resided here for over twenty years.

E. F. Larkham came to Dunn county in 1863 He is now Superintendent of Knapp, Stout & Co.'s lumber yard.

A J Brunelle, millwright, located at Menomonie in 1854, and has worked for Knapp, Stout & Co, ever since.

Carroll Lucus located at Mud Creek, in August, 1854 In 1855, he brought his family in his new home Here he remained on a farm until 1866, when the people of Dunn county spoiled a good farmer in order to have a good County Treasurer. This latter position he is still holding. He has also served four years as County Superintendent of Schools.

John Kelly, Jr., the present Register of Deeds, came to Dunn county in 1859 His regular business is farming

---·•·---

Religious Societies of Menomonie

THE CATHOLICS

THE church of the Emaculate Conception claims to be the first sectarian religious society of Menomonie. The church building was commenced April, 1861, under the direction of Father Sheriden; but it was not completed until 1865 The funds for building purposes were raised by the young men of the parish. A parsonage was erected in 1874. The present pastor is the Rev. Geo. Keller, diocese of La Crosse. The present trustees are Messrs. John Noulan, Peter Lamner and Thomas McKana. The parish now numbers about five hundred persons, and is in a thriving condition.

The Catholics here, as in many other places, are interesting themselves in the temperance cause—not to make a compulsory law, but to be the means of influencing people, by right of reason and self-respect, to take up on the temperance side. It is a good move, for the Catholics have the power to do more in putting down liquor drinking, than all the other societies combined, if they go rightly to work, and labor with a will — : .

METHODISTS

The society of the M. E. Church of Menomonie, was organized by Rev. S. Bowles, in the fall of 1857. The society, since 1857 to the present date, has been under the guardianship of the following Presiding Elders: Rev. S. Bowles, C. Hobert, M. Sorin, T. C. Golden, W. Cobbin, J. B. Raynolds and W. S. Wright. The following ministers have been the regularly appointed pastors to the society since its organization to the present date. Rev. W. N. Durnell, J. Gurley, J. Dyer, E. S. Havens till 1860. In 1861, J. B. Raynolds was appointed and his successors in office were D. P. Knapp, W. Woodley, W. Haw, T. C. Golden, W. W. Bashell, S. O. Brown, G. D. Brown, John Bell, E. S. Havens for the second time, and at the close of four months prosperous labor, Mr. Havens was transferred to the West Texas conference, and Rev. J. McClane was appointed at Menomonie. Six years from the organization of the society, its members numbered fifty. The highest number of members the society ever attained was ninety. It has at present seventy-five members. In 1864, the society organized a board of trustees; and in the spring of 1866 the building of the Centenary M. E. Church of Menomonie was commenced, under the direction of W. Wilson, A. J. Messenger and W. Haw, building committee. The church was finished and dedicated in 1867, at a cost of five thousand dollars, all contributed by the people. The growth and moral influence of this society have been various under the pressure of good or bad management, not always popular, yet ever seeking to maintain the spirit of primitive christianity, "peace on earth and good will to man." Under the preaching of its faithful pastors and in answer to the prayers of its devoted members, the altar of its church has frequently been crowded with earnest penitents. Here hundreds have been blessed, and have gone out from this society to become a blessing to the world.

The Sunday school of this society numbers eighty members, and is under the management of Mr. Joseph Gates, Superintendent, and his efficient corps of teachers The library of the school numbers some three hundred volumes. Seventy-six members of the school have signed and agreed to keep the following temperence pledge: " I hereby promise not to use bad words, either in or out of school; not to chew or smoke tobacco, and not to drink intoxicating liquors so long as I am a member of this school. So help me God, and keep me steadfast in the due performance of the same "—J McCLANE.

THE CONGREGATIONAL SOCIETY

Rev. John C Sherwin, an agent of the A. H. M. S., visited Menomonie in October, 1859, and endeavored to secure a missionary who would establish a Congregational society at this place.   His success, however, was not equal to his wishes: for it was not until December, 1861, that a society was organized.   This was under the ministry of Rev. Philo Canfield, who was one of the seven members that formed the organization.   In April, 1863, five more persons united with the church.   A month later, Rev. Philo Canfield resigned his care of the church, and the little flock remained without a shepherd until the fall of 1864, at which time Rev. F. M. Iams received a commission from the A. H. M. S. to preside over it.   Mr. Iams preached his farewell sermon to his church in November of the next year, on account of his having embraced the Baptist creed.   June 1st, 1868, Rev. John C Sherwin took the pastorate.   The members at the commencement of his labors, numbered only fifteen Services at this time were held in a small, unfinished building, now used as a private residence.   At the approach of winter, the Menomonie House Hall was secured for this purpose, and continued to be used by the society until the erection of the Congregational church, in 1870. This building cost nearly nine thousand dollars, and J. H. Knapp, Esq. was the prime mover in its erection.   It was dedicated October 21st, 1870.   The membership of the church now numbers eighty persons.—P.

GRACE CHURCH MISSION.

Episcopal service was first held in Menomonie in the summer of 1870, by Rev. R. F. Page of Eau Claire; and occasional service was held from that time until 1872, when a mission was organized under direction of Bishop Armitage In October of the same year the ladies formed a society, Mrs G H Birwise being president, Mrs. E B Bundy, vice president, Mrs. F. H. Weber, secretary, and Mrs R Macauley, treasurer. It was for the purpose of purchasing lots on which to erect a church and parsonage, which they succeeded in doing in March, 1873, completing their payments for the same in May, 1874. The whole sum paid for the lots was six hundred dollars, and was raised by the efforts of the ladies. A church that will cost three thousand dollars is now in process of erection.—B

FIRST BAPTIST CHURCH

The Rev. Mr. Pittman, who taught the first day school in Menomonie, and preached on the Sabbath, was a Baptist. In 1861, Rev. Amasa Gale, at that time the Baptist State Missionary, agent for Minnesota and a portion of Wisconsin, held a protracted meeting in Menomonie, resulting, by the blessing of God, in the conversion of several persons, Mrs Captain Wilson and others. It may be of interest to add, that Mr. Gale, having prosecuted with great success his work in Minnesota for sixteen years, in making the tour of Palestine, died in Joppa, November, 25th, 1871. Three weeks previous to his death, he preached a sermon and immersed one of his traveling companions in the Jordan, at the place where Jesus was baptized. A year subsequent to the above named protracted meeting, the Rev. Morgan Edwards, of Fort Madison, Iowa, held a series of meetings in Menomonie, resulting under God, in the conversion of a goodly number, who, together with some who were converted in the former meeting, were immersed by Mr. Edwards. The Menomonie First Baptist Church, was organized December 18th, 1864. But little, however, was done by way of sustaining public services, till October 1866, when the pastorate of W W. Ames, the present encumbent, commenced. At an early date, an article was incorporated into the church covenant, disfellowshipping all secret organizations, believing the principle of sworn secrecy to be incompatible with His gospel who said. "Ye are the light of the world, a city set upon a hill cannot be hid. Neither do men light a candle and put it under a bushel, but on a candlestick, that it may give light to all that are in the house." Another article was incorporated, discountenancing the manufacture, sale and use of intoxicating drinks, and pledging the church to the use of unfermented wine only, at the communion. The pastor preached every other Sabbath for two years, at the end of which time a neat and convenient chapel was dedicated for the use of the church in that place   At the same time, the pastor and his wife organized a Mission Bible School at Sherburne Prairie, five miles from Menomonie, August, 1867, which was superintended Mrs. Ames until the spring of 1871   Since that time, the school has been classified and carried on mostly by members of the Menomonie church, who, during the year 1870, built a beautiful chapel for the school and preaching services connected with it, which chapel makes a pleasant, attractive Sabbath home for the church-going people of the Prairie, and the means of healthful activity to members of the Menomonie church. It should be said that some of the Prairie people, and others, contributed towards the chapel, and that, financially, the school is self-sustaining. The Menomonie First Baptist Church organized its home school at Knapp, Stout & Co.'s hall, January, 1869   Capt. William Wilson was appointed Superintendent, and has served until the present time Some twelve hundred persons have belonged to the school, a large percentage of whom were children of foreigners.   Many of this number are now scattered over this state, and other states and territories, carrying with them the knowledge of bible truths, ' which are able to make them wise unto salvation," and cause "the desert to bud and blossom as the rose."

Capt Wilson, converted under the pleadings of Mr. Edwards, and with his wife and others immersed by him, sought and found admission to the church as early as January, 1863.   Believing that God put it in his heart to do so, he built and furnished, at his own expense, the beautiful house of worship now occupied by the church and school and which was dedicated March 12th, 1871. Rev. J. W. Fish, Baptist State Missionary Agent for Wisconsin, preached the dedication sermon, and continued to preach and assist the pastor in a series of meetings for two weeks, resulting in the addition of considerable numbers to the church   About a year afterwards, he labored in another protracted meeting, with marked results.   Thus the new house dedicated to God was immediately filled with tokens of the divine presence and power   Rev. C H Colver served as pastor one year, ending March, 1874.   The church and school have put in circulation a vast amount of Christian literature, which has been scattered abroad to bless many who otherwise would have been almost without religious reading   The church has passed through seasons of great apparent prosperity, and also of severe trial, but can say "hitherto hath the Lord helped us," and are resolved, by His aid, to defend and propagate "the faith once delivered to the saints."—W. W AMES

OLIVET BAPTIST CHURCH

A division having occurred in the First Baptist Church of Menomonie, the Olivet Baptist Church was organized May 12th, 1874, and was composed entirely of persons who had been members of the First Baptist Church. It is Calvenistic, having adopted the old New Hampshire confession of faith, as found in J. Newton Brown's Encyclopedia of Religious Knowledge. May 27th, 1874, it was in due form unanimously recognized as a regular Baptist Church, by an Ecclesiastical Council, called for that purpose, of which council Rev. T. E. Keeley of Hudson, was Moderator, and Rev. C. K. Colver, Clerk. At the ensuing meeting of the St. Croix Valley Baptist Association in Hudson, June 3d and 4th, 1874, the Olivet Church became a member of that body. It maintains regular public worship, and a Bible School in Olivet Hall, a place specially fitted up for these purposes. The Church is now under the pastoral care of Rev. C. K. Colver. The Superintendent of the Bible School is S. G. Dean. The Trustees are N. Barnhen, J. T. Long and L. L. Lukham. —c

———..——

Knapp, Stout & Company.

The firm which bears the name of Knapp, Stout & Co. deserves more than a passing notice, and though it necessarily figures largely in the history of Menomonie and Dunn county as already given, this work would be incomplete without a description of the great manufacturing institution which it represents. Those of our readers who have followed the history through, will remember how two young men who possessed little of this world's goods, but who had hands willing to labor, poled the keel-boat which bore them to their new home in the great wilderness; but the reader will not fully understand what a work this new firm has accomplished, or what a mammoth institution it is, until he has gone with us through the establishments and branch establishments which the company own, and sees the hundreds of men that are employed and the work that is done.

36

The present firm of Knapp, Stout & Co. comprises six members, four of whom reside in Menomonie. These are John H. Knapp Esq. Capt. William Wilson, Capt. Andrew Tainter, and T B. Wilson, Esq who is a son of Capt. William Wilson. The other two members are H. L. Stout, Esq who is in charge of the branch office at Dubuque, and J. H Douglass, Esq who superintends the branch office at St Louis

Knapp, Stout & Co have in Menomonie a large water power saw mill capable of sawing three hundred thousand feet of lumber every twelve hours during the season for manufacturing lumber, say from April 1st to Dec. 1st They have also a large steam saw mill, built especially for sawing long timber, and one of the largest and best flouring mills in the State, run also by water power. In connection with these Mills, they own and operate a foundry, machine shop, blacksmith and wagon shops. They make their own barrels for their flour mill and pork barrels for their pork house. They have an extensive harness shop for making and repairing their own harness used by the numerous teams employed in so large a business. They carry the most varied and extensive stock of merchandise to be found in the state outside of Milwaukee. Their shingle and planing mill in Menomonie is situated at the mouth of Wilson Creek, which empties into the main river about forty yards above their large water power saw mill

The lake or pond, made by the dam across the main Red Cedar river at this point, is one and a half miles long by about from three quarters of a mile to one mile in width; and gives easy boomage for two hundred and fifty million feet of lumber in the logs.

At Rice Lake, in Barron County, sixty miles north of Menomonie, they have a saw-mill and a grist mill, both run by water power, also a store, a hotel and a large farm. At Prairie Farm, also in Barron county, they have a water power saw-mill, a grist mill, a large store, and a farm of nine hundred and sixty acres, all under cultivation.— The above are both growing, active new villages, offering good openings for enterprising persons.

At Downsville, eight miles below Menomonie on the Red Cedar river, this Company has also a large water power saw mill and fine facilities for holding logs. In connection with the mills are the necessary shops, a large store of varied merchandise, and half a mile from the village of Downsville, a large and well regulated farm.

They have branch establishments not only at the points already named, but also at Dunnville in the same county, at Waubeck in Pepin county, at Read's Landing, Minnesota and at Dubuque, Iowa, where they have a large lumber yard and a saw mill. At St Louis Mo., they have also a large lumber yard, which wholesales lumber to Missouri, Kansas, Nebraska and other states and territories

At their various saw mills, during the year 1874, they sawed seventy million feet of logs into lumber and shingles

Knapp, Stout & Company employ in their lumbering operations from twelve hundred to fifteen hundred men They are said to be the largest manufacturers of lumber in the world, and the largest farmers in the state of Wisconsin. One of their farms, known as the Moore Farm, contains about two thousand acres, nearly all under cultivation They are extensive land owners, both of improved and unimproved lands, situated in Dunn and Barron counties, much of which is for sale Parties in search of new homes in the beautiful, healthgiving state of Wisconsin, or those in the state who are not pleasantly located and desire a change, would do well to see or write to this firm before purchasing elsewhere, as the company offer some very desirable farms, both improved and unimproved, at very reasonable rates Unlike some representative of wealth, the members of this company are always courteous and accommodating to all, and parties who might desire to visit them, or to write to them for information concerning the sale of lands, may be sure of a pleasant reception, and prompt replies

---

Jim O'Shaugnessey's Confession.

Arrah' is it in ravin' about ye,
   Whin me eyes shud be fastened in slape,
That I am to convince, widout doubt, ye
   That me love, like the oshun, is dape?
Must me lips be etarnally chantin'
   The charms I belave ye persess'
O, begorra, if lovin' is rantin,
   I am short of a crop, I confess'

Arrah! is it a sign of a lover,
 Ishpecially tinder and and true,
To be aloppin' one's agonies over
 In the way that some blunderheads do?
Musht he sit on the cold arth a watchin'
 The athurs, wid his eyes lookin' sad,
'Till a death cold perhaps he is catchin'?
 I confess that I will not, be dad!
Whin love's fed upon sorrers, so cruel,
 The warmhest affections soon tire!
How kin one on a water soaked fuel
 Hope to kape up an illigant fire?
Though yure virtues are many and glowin',
 As the numerous athurs of the sky;
Ah! the divil a bit use of showin'
 Them to one who's jist ready to die!
Health is love's hand maid, sure to me notion
 And nonsensical fudge the romance
Of a suckin' dove's cooin' devotion,
 Who kin nayther fight, fiddle nor dance!
Bah! of lover made up of disases,
 Pains, gripes and a de'il of a cough!
Ah! if such be the fellar that plases,
 I'll confess Jim O'Shaughnessey's off
Well I know, whin in courtship embarkin',
 Some consider it wonderful wise,
To so act in the business of sparkin',
 As if all its comforts were sighs;
And they try to convince ye that Coopid
 The blarney stone licks jist for spoort.
I confess now such practices stoopid
 Is not Jim O'Shaughnessey's foorte!
Some will swear yure complexion is clearer
 Than the wather that runs from a spring,
That yure leasht little finger is dearer
 To them than the hand of a king!
That their first thought of ye in the mornin'
 And the last one that gushes at night,
Is, that angels not often are born in
 This world to enrapture the sight!

Some will sware they could not live ten minutes,
  Unless ye shud answer them "Yea,"
That yure voice is as swate as a linnet's,
  And yure eyes jist as bright as the day,
That their hearts by untimely decay nipped,
  Would wither like frost bitten grass,
And the world be as dark as the old Agypt'
  I'll confess I'm not yet such an ass

To be brafe, since I mide me confession,
  I would like jist before I depart,
Some sort of a look or expression,
  That shall show me the state of yure heart'
If to spake out, yure mouth is not riddy,
  Ye might say in a delicate wink,
"Jim O'Shaughnessy's healthy and stiddy,
  And I'll marry the blubber—I think'"

There, since now ye has done it, och, honey'
  In this world there's no happier chap,
I will hunt it all over for money,
  And pour all that I get in yure lap
And I sware now, though greater or lesser
  Be the trials that harass me way,
Jim O'Shaughnessy's lady confessor
  Shall regret not her sly wink to day—

THEOPHILE THREE H, L?

—

Business Directory,
MENOMONIE, DUNN COUNTY, WISCONSIN

County Officers.
ROBERT MACAULEY, County Judge
NILS MICHELET, Clerk of Circuit Court
THOMAS J. GEORGE, Sheriff
H A. WILCOX, Under Sheriff.
R. C. BIERCE, District Attorney.
CARROLL LUCAS, County Treasurer.

W. H. LANDON, County Clerk.
JOHN KELLEY, JR., Register of Deeds.
THOMAS PARKER, County Surveyor.
GEORGE SCHAFER, County School Superintendent
J. P. WOOD, Coroner.

Town Officers.

A. O. BAILEY,
OLEUS OLSON,   } Supervisors
FREDERICK URSINUS.

THOMAS S. HELLER, Town Clerk.
GEO GALLAWAY, Town Treasurer
ROBERT MACAULEY, Assessor.

JACOB JUNGCK,
AMUND AMUNDSON,   } Justices of the Peace.
AUG. BALAND

E. L DOOLITTLE,
JOHN NOULAN,   } Constables.
H. D. RANSIER,

A H. JOHNSON, Scaler of Weights and Measures.

Professional Men.

ATTORNEYS

S. W. Hunt.	F. J. McLean,	E B Bundy.
C E. Freeman.	R C Bierce.	A J, Messenger.
Nils Michelet.		Robert Macauley.

PHYSICIANS

W C. Pease.	Charles C. Wadsworth,	W. F. Nichols.
J. M. Gates.		W. A. Bury

Banks.

S. B. French.   A Amundson.

Printing Office.

"Dunn County News." Flint & Weber, Editors and Proprietors.

Hotels.

Menomonie House	Merchants Hotel	Wisconsin House.
Union House		European Hotel.

Union High School.

J. B Thayer, Principal

Janet E. Stewart, Assistant

Libbie B. Thayer, Grammar Department

Hattie A Salisbury, } Intermediate Department.
Lottie S Walker, }

Lizzie Miller, }
Mary Yeo, }
Joseph H Gates, } Primary Department.
Mrs S W. Ritche, }

Churches.

Congregational, J. C Sherwin, Pastor.

Methodist Episcopal, J. McClane, Pastor

First Baptist, W. W. Ames, Pastor

Second Baptist, C K Colver.

Episcopal, (vacant)

Catholic, George Keller, Pastor.

Norwegian Lutheran, H Krog, Pastor

Scandinavian Lutheran, G Hoyme, Pastor

GENERAL BUSINESS DIRECTORY.

ANDERSON, H. A , Moulder with Knapp, Stout & Co.

Ames, W., Jr., Veterinery Surgeon.

Andress, Ira, Veterinery Surgeon

BONELL, FRED , Photographer, and dealer in Organs, Pianos, etc

Bunker, C. W., Carpenter and Joiner

Baird, W. H., Student at Law, with F J McLean

Blems, H. C., Contractor and Builder

Burch, N , Clerk with Knapp, Stout & Co

Barwise, G H., In charge of office department of Knapp, Stout & Co

Brewer, Geo. R , General Sup't Company's Clothing Department.

Brunelle, A. I , Millwright with Company

Burk, John A , Machinist with Company

Burke, Louis, Harness Maker with Company

Brayton, Orville, Land Agent

Burton, G. F., Pattern Maker with Company

Bull, Mrs S , Millinery and Dress Making.

Bunker, O A., Builder and Contractor

Bailey, A O , Dealer in Hides, Furs, Wool and Ginseng.

Belair, Adolph, Painter and Glazier.

Berger, Anton, Restaurant.

Bush, S. R., Blacksmith

Bailey, S J., Practical Mason and Bricklayer.

Bury, Dr W A , Eye and Ear Doctor.

CONDON, THOS , Grocer ; Thirty-fourth street

Chickering, F. Jr., Agent Perkins, Newhall & Perkins Woolens, Montello, Wisconsin.

Coleman, W. E , Cashier with Knapp, Stout & Co.

Clark, F M. Telegraph Operator.

Conway & Andrus, Milliners and Dressmakers

Cassidy, H T., Clerk with S. B French.

Clark, C A., Salesman with Company.

Christenson, Peter, Miller with Knapp Stout & Co

Cavanagh, John, Menomonie Marble Works

Carpenter, J , Millwright, with Knapp, Stout & C)

Diedrich, F., Harness Maker

Depew, A J., Millwright.

Dean, S. G., Agent for the Remington Sewing Machine.

Downs, W L., Lumberman.

Dahl & Embretson, European Hotel

Desprois, Joe, Express Messenger

Edwards & Son, Dealers in Hardware, Paints and Oils.

Edeberg, John, Miller with Knapp, Stout & Co

Egdahl, O. A., Foreman Company's Water Mill

Eytcheson, N C , Boots, Shoes and Groceries.

Evenson, Hans, Moulder with Company.

Ehrhard, Adam, Cooper

Ehrhard, Jacob, Cooper

Ehrhard, Louis, Cooper.

Eastwood, J R., Dealer in Pumps

FLINT, R J., " Dunn County News."

FRENCH, S. B , Banker, Merchant and Real Estate Agent, 34th St.

FOWLER, MRS G. M , Millinery and Furnishing Goods, 34th St.

FOWLER, G. M., Millwright and Surveyor

FOWLER, WILL, Music Teacher and agent for New England Organ.

Fritzsche, Paul, Grain Buyer.

Flynn, J C , Clerk Menomonie House.

Fletcher, Miss Eva, Book-keeper for A. O Bailey

Freeman. "Dug," "Devil" "News" Office

Flood, Wm , Blacksmith

Fuss. Chris, Brewer

Fussell, J H , Assistant Foreman in Company's Lumber Yard

GOODMAN, P A , Carriage and Wagon Maker

Gray, Irving, with Knapp Stout & Co

Grob, Otto, Clerk

Gordon, T E , Machinist with Company

Gallaway, George. Drayman

HOLMES, P C , Dealer in Furniture. Carpeting, etc

Hull, D S , Druggist, Thirty-fourth street

Hunt, Wescott. Grocer, Thirty-fourth street

Halfhide, M , Wagon Maker with Company

Heller, J A , Dentist

Hughes, J M , Brick maker

Heller, T S , Insurance Agent

Hughes, Lewis, Farmer

Hudson, W G , Carpenter

Hildebrandt Rev. W , Pastor German M E Church

Hart, Charles H , clerk George Tonnar's Drug Store

Jensen, Peter. Turner with Knapp, Stout & Co

Jensen, Andrew, Miller with Knapp, Stout & Co

Johnson, A H , Grocer and Livery Stable Proprietor

J Johnson & Co , Shoe Shop and Boarding House

Jungck, Charles. Boot and Shoe Maker

KNAPP, JOHN H , of Knapp, Stout & Co.

KNAPP, STOUT & CO , Lumbermen, Manufacturers and Merchants.

Knapp, H E , Book-keeper and Surveyor.

Kelley, Frank, & Co., Brick Makers.

Kent, William, Farmer.

Knoble, John, Wisconsin House

Kreiser, Joseph, Restaurant

Knutson. Charles. Saw Filer

LARKHAM, E F , Superintendent Company's Lumber Yard

Lyman, J , clerk with Knapp, Stout & Co

Landon, W. H , County Clerk

L Lamson & Co , Contractors and Builders

Lammer, Peter, Clothing Store, Main street

Larson, E , Merchant.

Lord, C D , Depot House

Lammer, Peter, Merchant Tailor.

Lucus, Herbert, Salesman with Wescott Hunt

McKAHAN, S. D , Postmaster

McKahan, J B., Wholesale and Retail Dealer in all kinds of Merchandise

Marks, E , Sup't Mercantile Department Company's Store,

Markham, S. F , Sup't Grocery Department Company's Store.

McClafferty, A , Sup't Tailoring Department Company's Store.

Marugg, Simon, with Knapp, Stout & Co.

McMoran, Thomas, Foreman Company's Harness Shop.

Miller, Jacob, Artist and Music Teacher

Mott, Mrs. M. L. Librarian.

Moss, T. F , Agent Florence Sewing Machine

Miller, C. E., Baker and Confectioner.

Manske, Ed , Meat Market.

Martin, G. F., Painter

Martin, J M Blacksmith.

Martin, B M., Planer.

NEWSOM, E J., Badger State Clubbing Agency.

Noble, N. B., Assistant Sup't Company's Business Office.

Nott, W. W , Contractor and Builder.

Nonnac, A., Carpenter with Knapp, Stout & Co.

Newsom, A. M., Clerk in Company's Flouring Mill.

Noulan, John, Lumberman.

Newsom Brothers, Apiary and Poultry Yard

ORDEMAN, G,, Paint Shop and Store.

Ohnstad, O , Boot and Shoe Store, Thirty-fourth street.

Olson, E , Billiard Hall.

Olson, Oleus, Contractor and Builder Shash, Doors and Blinds.

Overby, Christ, Jeweler

Parker, Thomas, Chief Surveyor for Knapp, Stout & Co

Parker, John, with Knapp, Stout & Co

Patterson, Adam, Machinist with Company.

Piers, Charles, Time-keeper for Company.

Pion, Lewis, Salesman with Knapp, Stout & Co.

Potter, H R., Salesman for S. B. French.

Prindle, M. D., Proprietor Durand and Menomonie Stage Line.

Pauly, Chris, Baker.

Pollard, W. B., Lumberman.

Pease, F E , Carpenter and Joiner.

Peterson, Holden, Salesman for J B McKahan

Quinn & Carmichael, Blacksmith and Wagon Shops

ROGERS, S. C , Sup't of Company's Boarding House

Robbins, J. B., Boot and Shoe Maker

Rogler, John, Tinner with Knapp, Stout & Co

Robinson, W C , Book-keeper

Roland, J E , Machinist

Reed, George, Baker with Company.

Romback, Phillip, Minnesota House

Ransier, H. D , Farmer.

SPRAGUE, J B , Proprietor of the Stage Line from Menomonie to Rice Lake.

Schroeder, Clark, Blacksmith with Company

Stone, T. S., Hardware Department of Knapp, Stout & Co

Stricker, F. M , Clothing Department of Knapp, Stout & Co

Solberg and Amundson, General Merchandise

Schutte & Quilling, Dealers in General Merchandise, and Proprietors of the Banking and Steamship Agency

Syverson, A., Boots and Shoes.

Sayles, Herbert, Barber, Thirty-fourth street.

Smveley, J. H., Dealer in Organs, Sewing and Knitting Machines

Scanlon, John, Wood Sawyer

Stendahl, Erick, Cook

Soper, G. C , Foreman for Company.

Sander, George H , Dry Goods Clerk

Swenomson, A., Farmer

Sherburne, A. C , Farmer.

Schwehm, Jacob, Restaurant.

Story, D. Restaurant.

Sprague, J. B , Mail Contractor

Stephens, John, Blacksmith and Carriage Shops.

Sherwin, W. A , Foreman "News" Office

TAINTER, CAPT. ANDREW, with Knapp, Stout & Co

TONNAR, GEORGE, Drugs, Stationery and Books, 34th street

Tainter, J B., City Livery.

Thorn, B. S., Wagon Maker

Tuttle, E. S.,

Toft, E A. Watch Maker and Jeweler.

Thomas, I. J , Architect, Master Mechanic and Bridge Builder.

Thompson, Geo. P., Telegraph Operator, Depot.

Voedisch, C., Furniture Store.

Voedisch, Chris., Restaurant.

WILSON, CAPT. WILLIAM, of Knapp, Stout & Co.

WILSON, THOMAS B., of Knapp, Stout & Co.

WEBER, E. H., of the " Dunn County News."

Woods, J. J., Druggist with Knapp, Stout & Co.

Warren, William, Blacksmith.

Waldron, J. E., Carpenter and Joiner.

Wasserer, Frank, Eagle House

Young, W. D. Lumberman.

Yeo, William, Miller with Knapp, Stout & Co.

Yeo, William, Jr Foreman Company's Flouring Mill.

How They Drop from Our Lives.

How the things that we love drop away from our lives
    As the beautiful flowers die ;
And some sweet, wayside blossom springs upward and thrives
    In the soil, where their ashes lie !

One by one, do they silently wither away,
    And in darkness we weep for our dead,
Never thinking the clouds will be lifted some day,
    And another one bloom in their stead ; —

Never thinking the sun of the morrow may be
    Just as bright as the sun of the past,
And the beauty next summer of flower and tree
    None the less for the winter's sharp blast.

How unwise, if a blossom we cherish should fade,
    To believe that all beauty is gone ;
Or when darkness is brooding on hill and in glade,
    To deny that a morning will dawn !

How unwise, when a loved one is false to his vow,
　Or a treasure is taken above,
To declare with a shadow of woe on our brow,
　That on earth there is nothing to love

True, the things that we love drop away from our lives,
　As the beautiful flowers die ;
But, thank God! some sweet blossom springs upward and thrives,
　In the soil, where their ashes lie.'—BELLA FRENCH

—— · · · ——

Playing Forfeits.

MATTIE was going to have some company, one evening It was in the beautiful summer time, a good many years ago. The house, where Mattie lived, was a white cottage in a village, but it had a pretty flower garden in front of it, and the little girls, and large ones too, loved to congregate there   But on this particular evening, Mattie's friends were invited guests for she was to have a supper party. Belle was the first one who came   She was fifteen years old and quite a young lady   There were two Marys, the oldest of which was called Mollie, in order to designate the two, one from the other   Helen and Sarah made up the half dozen   And what a gay half dozen girls they were! They lived for mischief, and mischief seemed to abound for them. The supper was eaten with a relish, and spiced, as it went down, with a wee bit of gossip; for our immature women partake considerably of their mother's dispositions. Betsey had been getting a new bonnet, Julia was going away to school, and, Alice had actually got a beau All of which had to be talked over and commented on.   When they were done eating supper, the girls cleared away the dishes and put the room in order for a game of forfeits   They played a long while, all of them, excepting Belle, having to pay numberless forfeits such as "chewing wood, "standing on chips, "measuring tape and the like and at last, Belle was caught

"Give her a hard one!" cried the rest of the girls to Sarah, who was the judge at that time.

"I have nearly exhausted my stock of forfeits," returned the one addressed "Let me see, what shall it be?" "Well Belle," addressing the prisoner, "you may go out in the street, and walk to the corner, quacking like a duck."

The girls laughed at the novel judgment. Belle laughed too, and ran out into the darkness to do as she was bidden, followed by all the girls, who wished to make sure that she did not deceive them in regard to the matter A great heavy cloud had spread over the sky, shutting out the twinkling stars, and causing the darkness to be very intense But Belle was not afraid of the darkness. Recklessly, she opened the gate, and went out.

"Quack! quack! quack!" she bawled, and the girls at the gate giggled. "Quack! quack! quack!" she yelled, louder than before, this time in the very face of a young gentleman, who was coming down the street, and whom the darkness had rendered imperceivable Belle caught one glance of his wondering eyes, then, frightened half out of her wits, fled back to the house to relate her strange adventure to the girls, who greeted it with roars of laughter What the gentleman thought of her behavior, Belle never knew, and the matter is a source of wonder to this day But, as I said before, it happened a good many years ago. The gay girls are all separated now Belle, who "loved not wisely, but too well," is leading a miserable life in a Southwestern State, with a brute of a husband, whom she once idolized, but now despises One of the Mary's is married and is an invalid, the other is an old maid Helen has been married, divorced, and married again

Sarah married Helen's first lover, and is unhappy, because she thinks her husband does not love her And Mattie, the spirit of mischief, who made life so bright to the other girls, who sang like a bird and danced like a fairy—Mattie, whom everyone thought would enjoy life so much, fell a victim to grief, through man's deceit, and died

Children, you are reveling in the golden sunshine of life. O, would that I might keep the storms away, that you might never know such woe as came to those six girls, who, on that summer evening, long ago, were playing forfeits —BONNIBEL.

Gems of Thought.

"Hate not. It is not worth while. Your life is not long enough to make it pay to cherish ill-will or hard thoughts toward any one. What if that man has cheated you, or that woman played you false? What if this friend has forsaken you in your time of need, or that one, having won your utmost confidence, your warmest love has concluded that he prefers to consider and treat you as a stranger? Let it all pass. What difference will it make to you in a few years when you go hence to the "undiscovered country?" All who ill-treat you will be more sorry for it then, than you, even in your deepest disappointment and grief, can be. A few more smiles, a few more tears, some pleasures, much pain, a little longer hurrying and worrying through the world, some hasty greetings, and abrupt farwells, and our play will be "played out," and the injurer and the injured will be led away, and ere long forgotten. Is it worth while to hate each other?"

"A man who hadn't much talent for conundrums, in attempting to get one off at a tea party at his own house, the other evening, got exceedingly mixed. He intended to ask the old question, "Why is a woman like ivy?" the familiar but gallant answer to which is, 'Because the more you're ruined the closer she clings.' But he put it, 'Why is ivy like a woman?' which none of the ladies could tell, and so the unfortunate man himself told them it was "Because the closer it clings the more you're ruined."

"Be not ashamed to confess that you have been in the wrong. It is but owning what you need not be ashamed of, that you now have more sense than you had before, to see your error, more humility to acknowledge it, and more grace to correct it."

"Words, 'those fickle daughters of the earth,' are the creation of a being that is finite, and when applied to explain that which is infinite, they fail, for that which is made surpasses not the maker, nor can that which is immeasurable by our thoughts be measured by our tongues."

"Never do a wrong thing to make a friend or to keep one. The man who wants you to do so is dearly purchased and at a sacrifice. Deal kindly and firmly with all men, and you will find it the policy which wears the best."

AN EPISODE OF THE LIQUOR WAR.

A fair crusader beseecheth Mr. Cobb Dollins to ascertain if any liquor is sold at the Restaurants, no saloons being allowed to exist.

He ascertaineth.

But concludes upon leaving the "Restaurant" that in union there is strength.

His testimony in the hands of the fair crusader, hurls vengeance at the head of the "Restaurant" man.

Immediately after he had a call elsewhere. and is helped away by the anti-temperance folks.

THE

American Sketch Book.

A COLLECTION OF

HISTORICAL INCIDENTS

WITH

Descriptions of Corresponding Localities.

HANDSOMELY ILLUSTRATED.

. . . .

EDITED BY BELLA FRENCH

——— . . .

—— . . .

LA CROSSE, WIS.
SKETCH BOOK COMPANY, PUBLISHERS
1874-5

.

INDEX TO VOL. I.

.

The American Sketch Book

is a historical magazine; which is at present engaged in giving the history of Wisconsin in monthly installments; each installment containing from fifty to sixty pages of reading matter, descriptive of some city, or village or county, i e giving the history, the advancement, improvement etc., of the place, together with one or more views, and biographical sketches of its prominent citizens, as well as a complete business directory.

Terms $2 50 per annum, that is $2 50 for twelve numbers Single copies thirty-five cents

A single line in the directory will be allowed each individual FREE OF CHARGE; for each additional line a charge of fifty cents will be made, and the same for inserting the single line in capitals

Advertisements for each number will be taken at the following rates: One page $12; half page $7; one fourth page $5.

No traveling agents employed The editor visits each place personally, and collects the material; also does her own canvassing and delivery of books A responsible local agent in every town is desired

---

LA CROSSE
Business College,
LA CROSSE, WISCONSIN.

Chicago, Milwaukee and St. Paul Railway.

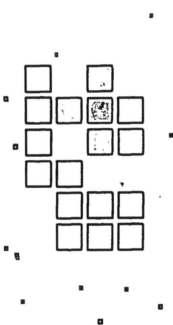

Lightning Source UK Ltd.
Milton Keynes UK
UKHW020651040621
384928UK00005B/346